FLOWERtripping™

A Traveler's Guide to What's Blooming When

Kate Savory

A SAVORY WORD

Chico, California

To Lana — Happy Flowertripping! Kate Savory —

FLOWERtripping™
A Traveler's Guide to What's Blooming When

Copyright © 2006 by Kate Savory

ISBN 0-9779216-0-3
First Edition: May 2006

Published by: A Savory Word
PO Box 1353 / Chico, CA 95927
www.asavoryword.com

All rights reserved. No part of this book may be reproduced by any mechanical, photographic, or electronic process, or in the form of a phonographic recording; nor may it be stored in a retrieval system, transmitted, or otherwise be copied for public or private use—other than for "fair use" as brief quotations embodied in articles and reviews—without prior written permission of the copyright owner.

Disclaimer
This book is designed to provide information about the subject matter covered. The subject matter presented has been obtained from independent sources and is designed to aid readers in formulating their own conclusions. Every effort has been made to ensure that the information is accurate at the date of publication. The author and publisher assume no responsibility for errors, omissions, or contrary interpretation. While the author believes that the information contained herein is accurate at the time of publication, readers should obtain independent advice and assistance to suit their circumstances.

Printed in the United States of America.

Cover art and design, text composition: Unique Word and Web Design
Printing: Digital Print & Design, Chico, CA

Library of Congress Control Number: 2006903021

Acknowledgements

A project like this doesn't happen overnight or single handedly, so I wish to thank the following people for their contribution to *FLOWERtripping™ A Traveler's Guide to What's Blooming When.*

To my parents, Rex and Jean Warden, who put up with all the tooth-picked sweet potatoes and avocado seeds rooting in jars on windowsills as I was growing up; to my sister, Carol Warden, who endured my constant litany, "oh, look at that one!" whenever we were hiking; and to my son, Scott Salzler, raised on our herb farm in New York, who has never doubted in the success of this project.

Big thanks also go to Margaret VanLaanMartin, Rene Boyes-Murdo, Sharon Ewing, Roseanne Apple, Billie Sommerfeld, and Sherrie Line-Coil (all members of my Dream Catchers mastermind group in Chico, California) for pushing me to get this project completed and out into the world. To Michelle Forner for her expertise in both coaching and editing and to Bev Rozendaal for her proofreading talents. Thanks also to Jessica Cummings, for being a printer par excellence, and to Michelle Olson for printing the display signs, banner and more.

Special thanks go to Bev and Jim Rozendaal, Katy Warren and Joanne Valentine for their encouragement.

My heartfelt gratitude goes to Billie Sommerfeld for her vision and talent in connecting *FLOWERtripping™* to travelers around the world.

And lastly, my deepest appreciation is for the support of my Soroptimist sisters in Chico, California.

Table of Contents

Foreword 7

Introduction 9

Section One LOCATIONS. . . . . 13 - 50

Section Two BLOOM TIMES . . . . 51 - 86

Section Three FLOWERS . . . . 87 - 127

Afterword. 128

FLOWERtripper! eNewsletter Information 131

About the Author 133

FLOWERtripping Tours 134

Foot Oil for *FLOWERtripping*™ 135

Book Order Information 136

Garden Tour Companies 137

My *FLOWERtripping*™ Notes 12, 50, 90, 128, 138

Foreword

"Come down to Kew, in Lilac Time,
It isn't far from London...."

For the English and flower-lovers worldwide, Kew is a name that poetic fantasy depicts as a special place of peace and repose, far from the noise and bustle of London. There one finds spacious areas replete with blossoms and sweet perfumes. Kew however is outstanding among world gardens, distinguished as the Royal Britannic garden, a UNESCO World Heritage site, and home to the world's largest collection of living plants. It is a global faunal laboratory.

Gardens have been tourist destinations for centuries and date to the earliest civilizations in the Middle East where horticulture first developed. Some of these early gardens survive, in adaptation, such as the Shalimar as a Mogul garden (in Lahore) and the other "baghs" of Pakistan and India. Later, in Europe, now-famous gardens were adjuncts to royal palaces for the enjoyment of the owners and their guests. As democratic ideas spread across the Continent in the eighteenth century, many of these gardens were opened to public view. The palace gardens at Fontainebleau and Versailles are two examples recognized as UNESCO World Sites. Although not so named, the five stately gardens of Japan share a similar history.

As modern tourism developed after World War II, some tour operators organized special garden tours, to take what are now termed *FLOWERtrippers* to view special gardens of Europe. Their special role emphasized the beauty and the sense of sanctuary that distinguished gardens from the urban scene. Thanks to their emphasis on home gardens, New Zealand hosts tours of civic and residential gardens during their down-under spring season. Similarly, tourist legions pour into the Netherlands for the annual tulip season. And floral oriented parades also attract large crowds, including Pasadena's 100-year-old New Year's Day parade featuring multi-national floats with an annual attendance of several million people.

The inherent need for information concerning floral events, displays, and geographic coverage could be greatly enhanced. Local garden clubs are active in many communities worldwide, but it appears there is no over-branching entity to coordinate their activities and to service the interests and needs of the *FLOWERtrippers.* In 1900 the USA National Audubon Society was founded; a century later there are 500,000 members who subscribe to and support their mission of information and conservation. With some 9,000 species extant, avid "birders" maintain "life lists" and seek opportunities to travel to often relatively inaccessible locations in search of exotic endemic birds. For them, "birding" is an avidly pursued avocation.

FLOWERtrippers may well represent another avocation but one that is until now only minimally supported. The publication of this path-breaking volume may well serve as catalyst for the creation of a flower-oriented botanical society. An appropriate name might be the Baschke Society, honoring Leopold and Rudolf Baschke whose 3,000 glass models created between 1887 and 1936 represent 840 floral varieties and is an internationally recognized collection at Harvard University. The Audubon Society similarly adopted their title to honor the scholarly contributions of bird-illustrator John James Audubon.

FLOWERtripping™ A Traveler's Guide to What's Blooming When is an innovative and signal addition to the travel literature and deserves public recognition and support.

Valene Smith McIntyre
May 2006
Editor, Hosts and Guests:
The Anthropology of Tourism
and founder,
TIM Tours
(Tours for Inquiring Minds)

Introduction

Want to attend the violet festival in France? Or see (and smell) the world's largest wisteria in bloom? Or view the carpet of wildflowers in Namaqualand, South Africa?

As a traveler, designing your itinerary is the first order of business when you feel the urge to take a journey. You can get very creative, depending on your available time and resources. Most people design their itineraries in this order:

1. They choose a destination.
2. They decide on a time frame.
3. They select specific sites to visit while they're at their destination.

FLOWERtripping™ A Traveler's Guide to What's Blooming When is a unique reference guide for travelers wanting to include flower sites in their itinerary. It is based on my years of researching flower books, guidebooks, tour itineraries, and related subjects on the Internet. *FLOWERtripping™* gathers destination-specific botanical information in one easy-to-read format for travelers.

The information in *FLOWERtripping™* is organized according to three criteria: **locations, bloom times,** and **flowers.** There are three ways to use this book:

1. Look up the country alphabetically in Section One to find what's blooming **there** and when.
2. Refer to the chart of bloom times in Section Two if you kno **when** you'd like to travel to a specific location.
3. Find out **what** flower is blooming where and when in Section Three.

For example: to help you decide when to travel to Machu Picchu for the best orchid display, look in any or all of the following:

1. **Section One, *Locations:*** Peru, Machu Picchu, May, orchids
2. **Section Two, *Bloom Times:*** May, Peru, Machu Picchu, orchids
3. **Section Three, *Flowers:*** orchids, Peru, Machu Picchu, May.

As travelers, we factor into our itineraries the "bookends" of travel: timing our trips to attend festivals (Mardi Gras), seasonal activities (the fall colors in New England), or special events (a new museum exhibit). Destination determinants can also be based on aspects most travelers would like to avoid, such as monsoons, or national/religious holidays. These are occurrences with a set time frame, things we do or do not want to miss if we're going to travel to this chosen destination.

This same approach can be extended to flowers and their blooming times: when I want to go to Tuscany, I select mid-May when the fields are full of red poppies. Going on safari in Kenya? The tissue flowers cover the Masai Mara in mid-January. Want to experience a laburnum arch in full bloom? Then you'll have to be at Bodnant Gardens in Wales in early June.

Use *FLOWERtripping*™ when planning your next trip to add the world's floral beauty to your itinerary. After all, it's the blooming wonders that make many flower trippers' journeys memorable. Wish lists might include experiencing the blue poppies in Bhutan, the black orchid in Madagascar, the silversword in Maui's Haleakala Crater, or the original African violets in Tanzania.

Flowers can greatly impact what we remember from our travels. Visually, their individual beauty (a single blossom on a Saguaro cactus in Arizona or a pink Jersey lily in the Channel Isles) or the impact of a mass of color (heather on the moors in Scotland or a field of pink, opium poppies in Tasmania) provides delightful mental triggers to refresh our memories of that trip.

Another effective memory stimulant is our sense of smell. The aroma that fills the air—a plaza of blooming orange trees in southern Spain, the "pizza" scented hills of Crete, a coffee plantation in Costa Rica, or Turkey's fields of roses grown for commercial rose oil—provides a powerful reminder of the entire trip when we're exposed to that fragrance again.

Need more inspiration? Participate with the locals at the Begonia Festival in Ballarat, Australia; the ritual cherry blossom viewing in public parks in Japan; or the Floating Flower Market in Amsterdam. There are so many flower festivals around the world, you could see one every month!

It's my hope that *FLOWERtripping*™ *A Traveler's Guide to What's Blooming When* will stimulate your travel dreams and add a new dimension to your next itinerary. Scan the information in this book for what intrigues you and select your next destination based on what's blooming when.

—Kate Savory,
Chico, California

My *FLOWERtripping*™ Notes

SECTION ONE

Locations

Going to Australia in October and want to know what's blooming where? Start with wildflowers and orchids in the Southwest and rhododendron in New South Wales. How about Bhutan in August? Edelweiss and other alpine wildflowers cover the high meadows that month.

There are botanical "hotspots" around the world with an abundance and variety of flowers: Australia, the Azores, Bhutan, Crete, Ecuador, Japan, Madagascar, South Africa, and Tasmania, to mention just a few. In fact, one botanical paradise, Madeira, is referred to as "the floating garden of the Atlantic."

These places have had the right combination of environmental conditions, geographic isolation, and plant genetics to develop their unique flora, both in quantity and diversity. A good number of the plants in these places are endemic, meaning they occur naturally there and nowhere else.

For *FLOWERtrippers* this means that when you visit these locations, there are many interesting plants blooming most of the year. For example, Ecuador has a variety of climate zones that accommodate orchids in the lowlands, bromeliads in the cloud forest, tropical flowers in the rainforest, a commercial rose crop in the foothills, and alpine wildflowers in the mountains.

For itinerary-planning purposes, selecting destinations based on what's blooming when means choosing locations that are known for their flowers—either their abundance or uniqueness.

In some locations, unique geological areas are accented by wildflowers. Places with dramatic scenery, such as Iceland, South Africa, Australia, and the moors of Britain, have thick carpets of seasonal flowers that not only frame the landscape but seem to soften its edges.

Other places serve as a backdrop to area flowers. Their presence adds visual significance to the site: the anemones blooming amid the ruins in the Karpaz Peninsula in Cypress; frankincense trees located in a rocky wadi outside Salalah, Oman; Darwin's cotton trees on Isabella Island in the Galapagos; and dogwood trees blooming among the giant sequoias in California's Sierra Mountains.

The combination of unique environment and flora occurs at the Burren on Ireland's mid-western coast. Picture this: the Gulf Stream determines the weather on the great limestone plateau, so Mediterranean and arctic wildflowers grow together in one natural landscape. Plants common to the southern regions reach their northern limits and plants common to the northern regions reach their southern limits. So alpine plants are growing here at sea level. It's like one-stop shopping for *FLOWERtrippers!*

Country	Location	Bloom Time	Flowers	Cultivated	Wild	Garden	Notes
Argentina	Bariloche/ Chalhuaco Valley	November to March	amancay (Alstroemeria)		open spaces		scented
Argentina	Bariloche	November to December	notro firebush		sandy areas, open spaces		
Argentina	Bariloche	November to December	fuchsia, wild		streamside		scented
Argentina	Bariloche	November to December	rosa mosqueta		throughout		edible products made from hips; scented
Argentina	Calafate	October to February	calafate		slopes		edible fruit, wine
Argentina	Calafate	December to March	sweet peas		open spaces, Glaciares National Park		scented
Argentina	Colon	December to March	petunias, wild		El Palmar National Park		site of original petunias; scented
Argentina	Patagonia/ Ushuaia	November	orchids		high plateaus, Tierra del Fuego National Park		scented
Argentina	Patagonia/ Ushuaia	November	violet, yellow		high plateaus, Tierra del Fuego National Park		scented

Country	Location	Bloom Time	Flowers	Cultivated	Wild	Garden	Notes
Australia	Brisbane	September to October	jacaranda trees			city wide	Goodna RSL Jacaranda Festival; scented
Australia	Grampians	October	bauera		streamside		
Australia	Grampians	October	wildflowers		throughout		scented
Australia	SW, Albany/ Margaret River	August to October	wildflowers		open spaces		bloom progresses from Pilbara to Esperance
Australia	SW, Albany/ Margaret River	September to October	orchids		throughout		scented
Australia	New South Wales/ Blackheath	late October to early November	rhododendron			Baccante Rhododendron Gardens	Blackheath Rhododendron Festival; scented
Australia	New South Wales	July to January	geranium, scented (Pelargonium)			gardens	scented
Australia	Victoria/ Ballarat	March	begonias			Ballarat Botanical Garden	Begonia Festival
Austria	Austrian Tyrol/ Seefeld	late June to July	alpine wildflowers		mountain meadows		
Azores	throughout	March to May	broom		open spaces		scented

Country	Location	Bloom Time	Flowers	Cultivated	Wild	Garden	Notes
Azores	throughout	June to August	sea lavender		coastal clifftops		
Belgium	Brussels	weekend of August 15th even years	begonias				Floral Carpet at Grand-Place (700,000+ flowers used)
Belgium	Ghent	late April	azaleas			city wide	scented
Belgium	Ghent	mid- to late April	daffodils, tulips			city wide	Floriales (floral display held every 5 years. Next is 2010)
Bermuda	throughout	April to May	Bermudiana		rocky areas,trails		
Bermuda	throughout	late March to April	lilies, Bermuda Easter			city wide	scented
Bermuda	throughout	April to July	oleander, (Nerium)		hedges		scented
Bhutan	Chele Le La	April	iris		upper cloud forest		scented
Bhutan	Dochula Pass	April to May	magnolias		middle cloud forest		scented
Bhutan	Dochula Pass	April to May	rhododendron		middle cloud forest		scented
Bhutan	high country	August	edelweiss		meadows		

Country	Location	Bloom Time	Flowers	Cultivated	Wild	Garden	Notes
Bhutan	high country	August	alpine wildflowers		mountain meadows		
Bhutan	Punakha	April	jacaranda trees			Punakha Dzong	scented
Bhutan	Thumshing La	April	daphne		upper cloud forest, Thumshing la National Park		scented
Bhutan	Paro, Thimphu	late May to July	poppies, blue		hillsides		scented
Bhutan	Thimphu, Thumshing La National Park	April	orchids		upper cloud forest		scented
Brazil	Amazon River Basin	most of year	lilies, giant Amazon		calm river inlets		scented
Bulgaria	Bansko	late June	alpine wildflowers		mountain meadows, Pirin Mtns National Park		
Bulgaria	Kazanlak	late May to early June	roses	fields in Valley of Roses			Festival of Roses, one of largest producers of rose oil; scented
Canada	British Columbia	late May to early June	violets		alpine areas		scented

Country	Location	Bloom Time	Flowers	Cultivated	Wild	Garden	Notes
Canada	British Columbia/ Golden	July	edelweiss	fields			extract used in skin care products
Canada	British Columbia/ Victoria	May to July	geranium, cranesbill			gardens	scented
Canada	Nova Scotia	May to June	rhododendron		rocky areas		scented
Canada	Nova Scotia	May to June	roses, wild		open spaces		scented
Canada	Nova Scotia	May to June	violets		bogs		scented
Canada	Nova Scotia	July to August	water lilies		lakes, ponds		scented
Canada	Ottawa	early to mid-May	tulips			city wide	scented
Canada	Quebec/ Grand-Metis	April	primulas			Reford Gardens	scented
Canada	Yukon	June to August	fireweed		open spaces		Territorial Flower
Canada	Yukon	June to August	heather, arctic		open spaces		burned as heating fuel (high resin content)
Caribbean	Bahamas	December	African tulip trees			throughout	
Caribbean	Bahamas	most of year	bougainvillea			throughout	scented
Caribbean	Dominica	April	Carib Wood trees		dry, coastal areas		

Country	Location	Bloom Time	Flowers	Cultivated	Wild	Garden	Notes
Caribbean	Dominica/ Roseau Valley	November	jade vines		rainforest	gardens	scented
Caribbean	throughout	May to October	frangipani		lowlands		scented
Caribbean	throughout	August to October	ylang ylang trees		humid lowlands		scented
Canary Islands	throughout	April	echiums		dry areas		
Channel Isles	Guernsey	April to June	orchids, wild	fields			scented
Channel Isles	Guernsey, Jersey	September to October	lilies, Guernsey, Jersey (Nerine)			gardens	Nerine Festival Guernsey; scented
Channel Isles	Jersey	April to May	foxgloves		coastal clifftops		scented
Channel Isles	Jersey	mid-June to mid-July	lavender	fields			scented
Channel Isles	Jersey	July	orchids		meadows, marshes		scented
Channel Isles	Jersey	September	autumn squill (Scilla)		coastal clifftops		scented
Channel Isles	Sark	June	bluebells		coastal clifftops		scented
Chile	between Valparaiso & Osorno	December to March	bellflower, Chilean		climbs trees in damp forests		National Flower

Country	Location	Bloom Time	Flowers	Cultivated	Wild	Garden	Notes
China	Guizhou/ Qianxi, Dafang	April	azaleas		natural azalea forest		Azalea Festival at Jinpo Village in Qianxi; scented
China	Beijing	April	crabapple trees			Temple of Heaven	scented
China	Beijing	April	wisteria			Hongluo Temple	scented
China	Guilin, Hangzhou, Shanghai	September to October	osmanthus, sweet			city wide	Osmanthus Festivals; scented
China	Hangzhou/ West Lake	May	peach trees			gardens	scented
China	Hangzhou/ West Lake	July to August	lotus			lakes	Lotus Festival; scented
China	Kunming	February	camellias			Golden Temple	camellia tree 500-800 years old; scented
China	Kunming	June to August	lotus			Beijing Summer Palace	Garden of Harmonious Interest; scented
China	Louyang	late April to mid-May	peonies			city wide	Peony Festival; scented

Country	Location	Bloom Time	Flowers	Cultivated	Wild	Garden	Notes
China	Nanjing	April	crabapple trees			Mochouhu Park	Flowering Crabapple Festival; scented
China	Nanjing	April	rhododendron		Damingshan Mtn.		Rhododendron Festival; scented
China	Shandong/ Yantai	late May	roses			city wide	Laizhou Rose Festival; scented
China	Suzhou	April	wisteria			Humble Administrator's Garden	scented
China	Wulingyuan	most of year	wildflowers		open spaces		scented
Corsica	throughout	March to April	gorse		hillsides		scented
Corsica	lower elevations	March to April	laburnum, wild		throughout		scented
Corsica	Evisa	early to mid-May	mint, Corsican		shaded areas, Forest of Aitone		scented
Corsica	Evisa/ Spelunca Gorge	early to mid-May	cyclamen		shaded areas		scented
Corsica	throughout	May	violets		alpine areas		scented
Corsica	throughout	May to early June	lavender, wild		hillsides		scented

Country	Location	Bloom Time	Flowers	Cultivated	Wild	Garden	Notes
Corsica	Venaco	early to mid-May	crocus, Corsican		upland valleys		scented
Costa Rica	Monteverde	late February to early March	bromeliads		Monteverde Cloud Forest Preserve		scented
Costa Rica	Monteverde	late February to early March	orchids (1,200 species)		Monteverde Cloud Forest Preserve		scented
Costa Rica	throughout	April to May	coffee trees	plantations			scented
Croatia	Hvar Island	June	lavender	fields			scented
Cypress	Karpaz Peninsula	late March to early April	anemones		hillsides		blooms amid ancient ruins; scented
Cypress	Karpaz Peninsula	late March to early April	orchids, bee		hillsides		scented
Denmark	Odense	June to August	fuchsias			Egeskov Castle, Kvaerndrup	scented
Denmark	Copenhagen	mid- to early June	tulips			Tivoli Gardens	scented
Ecuador	Cayambe	most of year	roses	plantations			scented
Ecuador	foothills	most of year	bromeliads		cloud forest		

Country	Location	Bloom Time	Flowers	Cultivated	Wild	Garden	Notes
Ecuador	throughout	February to April	orchids		lowlands & cloud forests		scented
Egypt	Cairo	June	Royal Poinciana trees (flame trees)			city wide	scented
Egypt	Cairo	June	jasmine, night-blooming			Mena House	scented
Egypt	Cairo	most of year	lotus, blue, (Egyptian)			Egyptian Museum forecourt pool	scented
England	Cornwall	March to June	blue quill		West Cornwall Coastal Path		
England	Cotswolds	early June	laburnum			Barnesley House	laburnum arch, scented
England	Devon, Yorkshire	August to September	heather		open spaces, moors		scented
England	North Devon	March t o June	daffodils		SW Coastal Path		scented
England	North Devon	May	bluebells		SW Coastal Path		scented
England	Hertfordshire/ St. Albans	late June to July	roses			Gardens of the Rose	scented
England	Isle of Wight	June to August	rock samphire		coastal clifftops		scented

Country	Location	Bloom Time	Flowers	Cultivated	Wild	Garden	Notes
England	Kent	late May	wisteria			Hever Castle	scented
England	Lake District	mid- to late May	heather			estate gardens	scented
England	Norfolk	late June to July	lavender	fields			scented
England	London/ Richmond Park	May	rhododendron			Isabella Plantation	scented
England	Stoke-on-Trent	mid-September	dahlias			Biddulph Grange Garden	
England	Surrey	May	bluebells		woodlands		scented
England	Wisely	late May to early June	azaleas			estate gardens	scented
England	throughout	most of year (March to May is best)	gorse		roadsides, open woodlands		scented
Estonia	Osmussaar Island	late June to early July	orchids		meadows		scented
Estonia	Saaremaa	late June to mid-July	wildflowers		Tuhu Bog, Puhtu Forest, Laelatu Meadows		
Ethiopia	Addis Ababa	September	daisy, Meskel		hillsides		
Fiji	throughout	June	orchids		throughout		scented
France	Arles	August	sunflowers	fields			

Country	Location	Bloom Time	Flowers	Cultivated	Wild	Garden	Notes
France	The Brenne, between Chatellerault & Chateauroux	mid-May	orchids		meadows, Cherine Natural Reserve		
France	Florac	June	orchid, monkey		Cevennes National Park		scented
France	Florac	June	rock rose		Cevennes National Park		scented
France	Dordogne/ Castaing	late May	fumana		meadows		
France	Dordogne/ Castaing	late May	globularia		meadows		
France	Dordogne/ Castaing	late May	meadow clary		meadows		
France	Dordogne/ Castaing	late May	orchid, military		meadows		scented
France	Giverny	mid- to late May	wisteria			Monet's Garden	scented
France	Grasse	mid-May	peonies			gardens	scented
France	Mandelieu	February	mimosa trees			city wide	Mimosa Festival; scented
France	Paris	April	lilacs			city wide	scented

Country	Location	Bloom Time	Flowers	Cultivated	Wild	Garden	Notes
France	Provence	mid- to late June	lavender	fields			scented
France	Pyrenees	mid-June	gentian		high meadows, Pyrenees National Park		scented
France	Pyrenees	June to July	daisies		meadows, Pyrenees National Park		site of original Shasta Daisy
France	Pyrenees	June to July	alpen rose (Rhododendron)		lake shores, Pyrenees National Park		scented
France	Pyrenees	June to July	iris, Pyrenean		Pyrenees National Park		scented
France	Pyrenees	June to July	ramondia		shady boulders, Pyrenees National Park		
France	Pyrenees	June to July	rock rose, Pyrenean		Pyrenees National Park		scented
France	Toulouse	February	violets			city wide	Violet Festival; scented
Galapagos	Isabella Island	May to November	Darwin's cotton		dry zone		

Country	Location	Bloom Time	Flowers	Cultivated	Wild	Garden	Notes
Galapagos	Plazas Island	May to November	portulaca		coastal areas		scented
Galapagos	Santa Cruz Island	May to November	daisy trees (Scalesia)		hillsides		scented
Greece	Crete	early to mid-April	tulips, wild lavender color		hillsides		scented
Greece	Crete	April	anemones		rocky outcrops		scented
Greece	Crete	April	daphne		rocky outcrops		scented
Greece	Crete	May to August	wild herbs (oregano, rosemary, sage, thyme)		hillsides		scented
Greece	Crete	September	dittany of Crete		Imbros Gorge		scented
Greece	Crete, Peleponnese	April to May	cyclamen		rocky outcrops		scented
Greece	Crete, Cephalonia, Paxos	May to early June	lavender, wild		open spaces		scented
Greece	Peleponnese	September to October	narcissus		rocky outcrops		scented
Greece	Peleponnese	October to November	crocus, purple		brushwood macquis		scented

Country	Location	Bloom Time	Flowers	Cultivated	Wild	Garden	Notes
Greece	Pindos	early to mid-June	foxgloves		Vikos Gorge		
Greece	Pindos	early to mid-June	orchids		Vikos Gorge		scented
Greece	Pindos	early to mid-June	ramondia		Vikos Gorge		
Greece	Skopelos	April to May	freesias	fields			scented
Greece	throughout	June	chamomile		open spaces		scented
Greece	throughout lower elevations	June	jasmine, night-blooming			gardens	scented
Greece	throughout	June	bougainvillea			gardens	scented
Holland	Amsterdam, Aalsmeer, Limmen	most of year	daffoldils, tulips, hyacinths	fields		Keukenhof Exhibition, Hortus Bulborum	Floating Flower Market, Aalsmeer Flower Auction (year 'round)
Iceland	throughout	June	cotton grass		wet areas		
Iceland	throughout	June	violets		open spaces		scented
Iceland	throughout	June to July	bluebells		open spaces		scented
Iceland	throughout	June to August	lupines		open spaces		scented

Country	Location	Bloom Time	Flowers	Cultivated	Wild	Garden	Notes
Iceland	throughout	June to August	primulas		open spaces	gardens	scented
Iceland	throughout	July	poppies: Iceland, arctic		open spaces		scented
Iceland	throughout	July to August	heather, arctic		open spaces		heather oil used in local spas
India	Coorg	March to May	coffee trees	plantations			scented
India	Sikkim	May to October	poppies, blue		hillsides		scented
India	Sikkim	May to October	primulas		hillsides		scented
India	Sikkim	May to October	rhododendron, magnolias		hillsides		60' tall rhododendron trees; scented
India	Sikkim, Gangtok	September to December	orchids, 454 species			Orchidarium & Orchid Sanctuary	Flower Exhibition Center; scented
India	South India	most of year	lotus			water gardens	National Flower; scented
India	Yumthang	May to June	alpine wildflowers		valleys		
India	Yumthang	May to June	rhododendron		valley, Singbha Rhododendron Sanctuary		scented

Country	Location	Bloom Time	Flowers	Cultivated	Wild	Garden	Notes
Iran	Khorasan Province	late October	crocus, saffron	fields			scented
Ireland	Burren	June to July	geranium, cranesbill		throughout		scented
Isles of Scilly	throughout	March to May	pansy, dwarf		coastal areas		scented
Isles of Scilly	throughout	late September to early April	narcissus	fields			scented
Israel	Mt. Gilboa	March	iris, Gilboa		hillsides		scented
Israel	Galilee	February	wildflowers		Atzmon Mtn to Yodfat Ridge		
Italy	Alta Badia	June to late August	daphne		Dolomites		scented
Italy	Alta Badia	June to late August	lilies, Turk's Cap		Dolomites		
Italy	Alta Badia	June to late August	morning glory		Dolomites		scented
Italy	Alta Badia	June to late August	rhododendron		Dolomites		scented
Italy	Piedmont/ Asti	June to July	basil	fields			scented
Italy	Tuscany, Umbria	mid-May	poppies, red		open spaces		scented

Country	Location	Bloom Time	Flowers	Cultivated	Wild	Garden	Notes
Japan	Chita City	late February to early March	plum trees		Sori Pond		Sori-iki Plum Blossom Festival (1,800 trees); scented
Japan	Gamagori City	June	hydrangea			Katahara Hot Springs	Hydrangea Festival; scented
Japan	Hiroshima/ Fukuyama	May	roses			city wide	City of Roses, Rose Festival; scented
Japan	Hokkaido	mid- to late May	tulips	fields			Kamiyubetsu Tulip Park Fair (1 million bulbs); scented
Japan	Hokkaido/ Furano	July to August	lavender	fields			scented
Japan	Kyoto/ Kita Ward	early April	camellias			Jizoan Temple	scented
Japan	Kyoto	early April	cherry trees			Byodo-in Temple, Fushimi Momoyama Castle, Heian Jingu Shrine	scented
Japan	Kyoto	late June to August	lotus			Hokogoin Temple	scented

Country	Location	Bloom Time	Flowers	Cultivated	Wild	Garden	Notes
Japan	Nara	early April	cherry trees			Nara Park, Kofukuji Temple	scented
Japan	Nara/ Tenri City	May	azaleas			Chogakuji Temple	scented
Japan	Osaka/ Ikeda City	mid-May	peonies			Kyuanji Temple	scented
Japan	Shimane/ Muika-ichiTown	early April	violets			city wide	Violet Festival; scented
Japan	Shimane/ Goka Village	late May	rhododendron			Murakamiki Oki Rhododendron Park	scented
Japan	Tokyo	late March to mid-April	cherry trees			estate gardens, Ueno Oncho Park, Shinjuku Gyoen	scented
Japan	Tokyo	late April to early May	wisteria			Kameido Tenjin Shrine	100 plants on 15 trellises planted 320 years ago
Japan	Tokyo/ Iriya	early July	morning glory			Kishibojin Shrine	Morning Glory Festival & Market; scented
Japan	Takeda City, Saga	late March	cherry trees			more than 2,500 sakura trees	Okajo Koen Cherry Blossom Festival; scented

Country	Location	Bloom Time	Flowers	Cultivated	Wild	Garden	Notes
Japan	Toyohashi City/ Kamo cho	June	iris			Kamo Nurseries, estate/Kamo Shrine	1,500 varieties, 39,000 in bloom; Iris Festival; scented
Japan	Yabu-gun	early April	magnolias			Koshoji Temple	scented
Japan	Yoshino Mtn.	mid-April	cherry trees, white		Kumano National Park		sequential blooming of centuries-old trees; scented
Java	throughout	early September	coffee trees	plantations			scented
Jordan	Madaba	April	gladiola, wild		hillsides		scented
Jordan	Madaba	April	iris, black		hillsides		scented
Jordan	Petra	June to July	oleander, wild		wadis		scented
Kenya	Nairobi area	most of year	bougainvillea			Karen Blixen House, Outspan Country Club, Mt. Kenya Safari Club	scented
Kenya	Masai Mara	January	tissue flowers		open spaces		
Korea	Gwangyang/ Maehwa Village	mid-March	apricot trees		hillsides		Apricot Festival; scented

Country	Location	Bloom Time	Flowers	Cultivated	Wild	Garden	Notes
Madagascar	coastal areas	September	Fish Poison Tree (Barringtonia)		along shores		scented
Madagascar	throughout	December to January	orchids, black			gardens	scented
Madagascar	Nosy Be	most of year	ylang ylang trees	plantations			scented
Madeira	Funchal	most of year	azaleas			city wide	scented
Madeira	Funchal	most of year	bougainvillea			city wide	canopy over river running through city; scented
Madeira	Funchal	most of year	fennel		hillsides		scented
Madeira	Funchal	most of year	hydrangeas		lines the road to Encumeada Pass		scented
Madeira	Funchal	most of year	jacaranda trees			city wide	scented
Madeira	throughout	most of year	lavender, wild		hillsides		scented
Madeira	Funchal	November to April	camellias			Quinta do Palheiro Ferreiro	scented
Madeira	Funchal	January to June	lilies, arum			city wide	scented
Madeira	throughout	January to July	echiums (Pride of Madeira)		open spaces		scented
Madeira	Funchal	February to April	freesias			city wide	scented

Country	Location	Bloom Time	Flowers	Cultivated	Wild	Garden	Notes
Madeira	throughout	mid-March to mid-May	fuchsias		along levadas		scented
Madeira	throughout	mid-March to mid-May	mimosa trees		along levadas		scented
Madeira	Funchal	April	wisteria			city wide	scented
Madeira	Funchal	April to June	proteas			gardens	
Madeira	throughout	early to mid-May	violets		alpine areas		scented
Madeira	Funchal	May to June	lilies, Madonna			city wide	scented
Madeira	Funchal	May to June	orchids		hillsides	gardens	scented
Madeira	throughout	June to October	frangipani (Plumeria)		lowlands	city wide	scented
Madeira	Funchal	September to November	lilies, belladonna			city wide	scented
Madeira	Funchal	September to November	lilies, Guernsey, Jersey			city wide	scented
Madeira	Funchal	October to February	poinsettias			city wide	
Malaysia	throughout	most of year	hibiscus		rainforest	gardens	National Flower; scented
Malaysia	Penang	September	orchid, giant		lowland rainforest	Bukit Jambul Orchid, Hibiscus, Reptile Gardens	scented

Country	Location	Bloom Time	Flowers	Cultivated	Wild	Garden	Notes
Malaysia	Sabah	April to early July	orchids		Mt. Kinabula National Park		scented
Malta	throughout	April to June	poppies		open spaces		scented
Malta	throughout	June to August	sea lavender		coastal clifftops		
Mexico	Chiapas	December	bromeliads			cloud forest	
Mexico	San Miguel de Allende	March	jacaranda trees			city wide	scented
Mexico	Tabasco	most of year	cacao trees	groves			source of chocolate
Mexico	Taxco	December	poinsettias		hillsides		site of original poinsettias
Mongolia	Northern	May to July	geranium, cranesbill		meadows		scented
Morocco	Atlas Mtns	most of year	lavender, wild		hillsides		scented
Morocco	Essaouira	April to May	argan trees		valleys		goats climb into trees to eat leaves when in bloom
Morocco	Kelaa/ Dades Valley	May to June	roses	fields			Rose Festival; scented
Nepal	Eastern	May to August	poppies, blue		hillsides		scented
Nepal	Western	July to August	poppies, blue	alpine areas			scented

Country	Location	Bloom Time	Flowers	Cultivated	Wild	Garden	Notes
New Zealand	Alexandra	September to November	wildflowers		Pisa or Flat Top Hill Conservation Reserve		scented
New Zealand	Auckland	November	roses			Parnell Gardens	Parnell Rose Festival; scented
New Zealand	Chatham Islands	September to October	forget-me-nots, Chatham Island		coastal clifftops, Henga Scenic Reserve, Kaingaroa Point		scented
New Zealand	New Plymouth	late October to early November	rhododendron			city wide	Taranaki Rhododendron Festival; scented
New Zealand	Otago	December to mid-February	alpine wildflowers		hillsides		
New Zealand	Rotorua	late October to mid-November	azaleas			city wide	scented
New Zealand	Rotorua	late October to mid-November	magnolia			city wide	scented
New Zealand	throughout	September to October	Kowhai trees		streamside, forest edges, nature parks		
New Zealand	Napier, Kaikoura, Waikato	January	lavender	fields			scented

Country	Location	Bloom Time	Flowers	Cultivated	Wild	Garden	Notes
Norway	Golsfjellet	mid- to late July	orchids		bogs		scented
Norway	Golsfjellet	mid- to late July	alpine wildflowers		mountain meadows		
Norway	Hardangerfjord	May	apple, pear, plum, cherry trees	orchards			scented
Oman	Dhofar/ Salalah	April	frankincense trees		rocky areas/ Wadi Qahshan		frankincense souq
Peru	Lima	most of year	bougainvillea			city wide	scented
Peru	Machu Picchu, Aguas Calientes	most of year, late April to June is best	orchids		along Inca Trail & at Machu Picchu	hotel gardens	scented
Peru	Urubamba Valley	January	lupines		open spaces		scented
Philippines	throughout	most of year	jasmine		rainforest	gardens	National Flower; scented
Philippines	throughout	most of year	ylang ylang trees		humid lowlands	city wide	scented
Portugal	Algarve	mid-January to February	almond trees	orchards			scented
Portugal	Algarve	April	pimpernel, blue		Sagres Point		
Portugal	Algarve/ Monchique	April	sea pinks (thrift)		Sagres Point		scented

Country	Location	Bloom Time	Flowers	Cultivated	Wild	Garden	Notes
Portugal	Serra da Arrabida	March	daffodils, wild		shady hillsides		scented
Puerto Rico	throughout	most of year	hibiscus		rainforest	gardens	scented
Sardinia	Fonni	early May	peonies, wild		hillsides		scented
Scotland	throughout	July	bluebells		open spaces		scented
Scotland	throughout	mid-August to early September	heather		hillsides, moors		National Heather Centre, Cherrybank, Perth; scented
Scotland	Harris Isle	April to May	orchids		open spaces		scented
Scotland	Isle of Iona	June to September	fuchsias		hedges		scented
Scotland	lowlands	August to September	thistle, Scotch		open spaces		National Flower
Sicily	coastal areas	May to June	geranium, scented (Pelargonium)		open spaces		scented
Slovakia	Carpathian Mtns	June	columbines		Low Tatras National Park		scented
Slovakia	Carpathian Mtns	June	daphne		High Tatras National Park		scented

Country	Location	Bloom Time	Flowers	Cultivated	Wild	Garden	Notes
Slovakia	Carpathian Mtns	June	iris, Siberian		steppes, Slovak Raj National Park		scented
Slovakia	Muran Plateau	June	orchids		Muranska National Park		scented
Slovenia	Julian Alps/ Ukanc	July	alpine wildflowers		mountain meadows		
South Africa	Limpopo & Western Cape	September to February	geranium, scented (Pelargonium)		sheltered areas in mountains		scented
South Africa	Namaqualand	July to September	daisies & wildflowers		Skilpad Reserve		
South Africa	Pretoria	September to October	jacaranda trees			city wide	"Jacaranda City;" scented
South Africa	southwestern Cape area	December	proteas	fields			
Spain	Alhambra	April to June	roses			gardens	scented
Spain	Camino de Santiago	April to May	violets		hillsides		scented
Spain	Camino de Santiago	May to June	wild herbs (lavender, rosemary, thyme) & wild roses		hillsides & along trail		scented

Country	Location	Bloom Time	Flowers	Cultivated	Wild	Garden	Notes
Spain	Castilla la Mancha	mid-October	crocus, saffron	fields			scented
Spain	Ordesa	June	butterworts		Ordesa National Park		
Spain	Ordesa	June	pansy, horned		Ordesa National Park		scented
Spain	Picos de Europa	June	columbines		Fuente De		scented
Spain	Picos de Europa	June	heather		hillsides		scented
Spain	Picos de Europa	June	orchids		meadows		scented
Spain	Picos de Europa	June	pasqueflowers		meadows		
Spain	Picos de Europa	June	sea holly		rocky areas		
Spain	Seville	April to May	orange trees			city wide, plazas	scented
Sweden	Lake Malaren	April to May	primulas		meadows		scented
Sweden	Oland	early to mid-June	orchids		Schaferi Meadows		scented
Switzerland	Swiss Alps/ Upper Engadine Valley	July	alpine wildflowers		mountain meadows		
Tasmania	Scottsdale	December	lavender	fields			scented

Country	Location	Bloom Time	Flowers	Cultivated	Wild	Garden	Notes
Tasmania	Scottsdale	December	poppies, pink opium	fields			scented
Tasmania	Wynyard	early October	tulips	fields			Wynyard Tulip Festival; scented
Tanzania	Ngorogoro Crater	early February	coffee trees	plantations			scented
Tanzania	Tanga/ Usambara Mtns	September to March	African violets (Saintpaulia)		rainforest, Amani Nature Preserve		site of original African violets
Thailand	Lopburi, Saraburi	November to February	sunflowers	fields			
Thailand	Loei Province	February	roses		Phu Kradung National Park		scented
Turkey	Cappadocia	late March to early April	cherry trees		Goreme National Park		scented
Turkey	Manisa	late May to early June	tulips		Mt. Spil National Park		site of original tulips; scented
Turkey	Miletus	May	poppies: purple, red, white		meadows		scented
Turkey	Taurus Mtns/ Isparta	late May to early July	roses	fields			Carpet & Rose Festival (July), one of largest producers of rose oil; scented

Country	Location	Bloom Time	Flowers	Cultivated	Wild	Garden	Notes
Turkey	Western & Central	late May to early June	daisies		open spaces		
US	Alaska	late May to late June	lousewort, wooly		rocky areas, tundra		
US	Alaska	late May to August	forget-me-nots		meadows		State Flower; scented
US	Alaska, SE & S Central	mid-June to mid-July	lilies, chocolate		coastal meadows		
US	Arizona/ Phoenix	April	jacaranda trees			city wide	scented
US	Arizona/ Tombstone	April	rose tree			arbor, Rose Tree Inn Museum	"oldest rose tree in the world" (8,000sqft arbor); scented
US	Arizona/ Tucson	May	saguaro cactus		hillsides, open spaces, Saguaro National Park	city wide	scented
US	California/ Carlsbad	early March to early May	ranunculus	fields			Flower Fields
US	California/ Chico	mid-February	almond trees	orchards			California Nut Festival; scented
US	California/ Death Valley	mid-March to mid-May	daisies, Panamint		valley floor		

Country	Location	Bloom Time	Flowers	Cultivated	Wild	Garden	Notes
US	California/ Ft. Bragg	April to mid-May	rhododendron			Mendocino Coast Botanic Garden	scented
US	California/ Lancaster	April	poppies, California		Antelope Valley Poppy Reserve		California Poppy Festival; scented
US	California/ Pasadena	January to February	camellias			Descanso Gardens	Camellia Festival; scented
US	California/ Sacramento	April	wildflowers		Mather Field		vernal pools: wildflowers in a unique ecosystem
US	California/ San Marino	February to April	bulbs, South Africa (clivias, gladioli)			Huntington Botanical Garden	scented
US	California/ Sierra Mtns	late May to late June	dogwoods		Sequoia & Kings Canyon National Park		among giant Sequoia trees; scented
US	California/ Sierra Madre	March	wisteria			city park	"largest blooming plant in the world" (500' branches), Wisteria Festival; scented

Country	Location	Bloom Time	Flowers	Cultivated	Wild	Garden	Notes
US	Colorado/ Vail	June to August	alpine wildflowers		mountain meadows	Betty Ford Alpine Gardens	world's highest botanical garden (8,200')
US	Colorado	May to August	columbines		mountains, foothills	gardens	scented
US	Colorado/ Dolores Canyon	May	phlox		foothills, canyons		scented
US	Florida/ Miami	mid-May to June	Royal Poinciana trees (flame trees)			city wide	Royal Poinciana Festival; scented
US	Georgia/ Savannah	mid- to late April	wisteria		covering trees	city wide	scented
US	Hawaii	most of year	bougainvillea			throughout	purple color; scented
US	Hawaii	May to October	frangipani (Plumeria)		lowlands	city wide	used in leis; scented
US	Hawaii	May	jacaranda trees			city wide	scented
US	Hawaii	October to February	proteas	fields		gardens	
US	Hawaii	August to October	ylang ylang trees		humid lowlands	gardens, parks	scented
US	Hawaii/ Maui	August to December	silversword		Haleakala National Park		grows only inside this crater

Country	Location	Bloom Time	Flowers	Cultivated	Wild	Garden	Notes
US	Kansas/ Goodland	August	sunflowers	fields			State Flower
US	Louisiana/ New Orleans	most of year	jasmine & night-blooming jasmine			city wide	scented
US	Michigan/ Holland	mid-May	tulips	fields			Holland Tulip Festival; scented
US	Michigan/ Mackinac Island	June	lilacs			gardens	Lilac Festival; scented
US	Mississippi/ Natchez	May to June	magnolias			city wide	scented
US	Missouri/ Ozarks	late May to October	coneflower, purple	fields	meadows, prairies		medicinal
US	Missouri/ St. Louis	June to July	caperbush			Missouri Botanical Garden	
US	Montana	May to June	lilies, yellow glacier		low valleys, east side of Glacier National Park		scented
US	Montana/ Blackfeet Highway	June to August	Indian paintbrush		meadows		
US	New York/ Rochester	mid-May	lilacs			Highland Park	Lilac Festival; scented

Country	Location	Bloom Time	Flowers	Cultivated	Wild	Garden	Notes
US	North Carolina/ Bakersville	mid-June	rhododendron, wild		Roan Mtn		Rhododendron Festival; scented
US	North Carolina/ Wilmington	early to mid-April	azaleas			Airlie Gardens, Orton Plantation	NC Azalea Festival; scented
US	North Carolina/ Fayetteville	late April	dogwoods			city wide	Dogwood Festival & dogwood trail; scented
US	Oregon/ Canby	August to September	dahlias	fields			Swan Island Dahlia Festival
US	Oregon/ Portland	June	roses			city wide, parks	City of Roses, Rose Festival; scented
US	Oregon/ Salem	mid-May to early June	iris	fields		Schreiner's Iris Gardens	scented
US	Rhode Island/ Kingston	mid-May	crabapple trees	orchard/ University of Rhode Island			East Farm Crabapple Festival; scented
US	South Carolina/ Charleston	February to April	azaleas			Middleton Place Plantation	scented

Country	Location	Bloom Time	Flowers	Cultivated	Wild	Garden	Notes
US	South Carolina/ Charleston	March to April	camellias			Magnolia & Middleton Place Plantation	oldest camellias in No. America; scented
US	Texas	June to September	bluebells		open spaces		scented
US	Texas/ Austin	late March to early April	bluebonnets		open spaces	San Antonio Botanical Garden	scented
US	Washington, DC	late March to early April	cherry trees			Tidal Basin	National Cherry Blossom Festival; scented
US	Washington/ Sequim	late June to August	lavender	fields			Sequim Lavender Festival; scented
US	Wyoming	July to August	lupines		meadows, Grand Teton National Park		scented
Vietnam	throughout	most of year	lotus		lakes & ponds		National Flower; scented
Wales	North Wales	early June				Bodnant Gardens	laburnum arch; scented
Wales	Shell Island	June			banks of estuary		scented
Wales	South Pembrokeshire/ Tenby	late February to early April	daffodils, Tenby		old church yards		scented

My *FLOWERtripping*™ Notes

SECTION TWO
Bloom Times

Can't get to Holland to see the tulips this spring? Catch them in Tasmania in October! Miss the blooming fields of lavender in June in Provence? No problem! You can see them in Japan in July or Tasmania in December.

This issue is a pivotal point of itinerary planning for *FLOWERtrippers:* researching bloom times for your next trip. It's the "when" of destination research and it is more than just which hemisphere and what season.

The bloom times of flowering plants are affected by many things, including the climatic determinates of the previous season (late spring, excess rainfall, drought, etc.), however, they also have an established pattern for blooming in their location.

Festival times are one of the best ways to determine the flora of an area. If there's a festival for a flower, its bloom time is fairly predictable. So a good focal point for *FLOWERtrippers* in planning their itinerary is finding out the month the festival is held.

The violet festivals in France and Japan and the lilac festivals in New York and Michigan compete with the Mimosa Festival in France, the Crabapple Festival in Nanjing, the Rhododendron Festival in Australia, and the Iris Festival in Japan. There's a flower festival somewhere around the world every month!

In certain latitudes, some flowers bloom almost year 'round (bougainvillea, jasmine, orchids), so you can be assured of a good floral display whatever time you choose. In addition, these places almost always have some unusual flower that you can plan your trip around. For example, the ylang ylang plantations on Nosy Be, Madagascar, bloom most of the year, so enjoying their intense aroma and beautiful flowers would already be on your itinerary when you travel to the island to see the black orchid, which only blooms from December to January.

Except for areas near the equator, spring is the premier flower season around the world. Timing your travels to include the floral display at your destination can increase your enjoyment of your trip. If you go to Kunming, China, in the spring you'll want to see the 500 to 800 year-old camellia tree at the Golden Temple in bloom—in February. While you're there, you can also view the fruit trees in bloom, particularly plum trees. Because plum blossoms are associated with the Chinese New Year, there's sure to be a plum flower festival nearby!

Bloom Time	Counry	Location	Flowers	Cultivated	Wild	Garden	Notes
January	Kenya	Masai Mara	tissue flowers		open spaces		
January	New Zealand	Napier, Kaikoura, Waikato	lavender	fields			scented
January	Peru	Urubamba Valley	lupines		open spaces		scented
January to February	US	California/ Pasadena	camellias			Descanso Gardens	Camellia Festival; scented
mid-January to February	Portugal	Algarve	almond trees	orchards			scented
January to June	Madeira	Funchal	lilies, arum			city wide	scented
January to July	Madeira	throughout	echiums (Pride of Madeira)		open spaces		
February	China	Kunming	camellias			Golden Temple	camellia tree 500-800 years old; scented
February	France	Mandelieu	mimosa trees			city wide	Mimosa Festival; scented
February	France	Toulouse	violets			city wide	Violet Festival; scented
February	Israel	Galilee	wildflowers		Atzmon Mtn to Yodfat Ridge		

Bloom Time	Counry	Location	Flowers	Cultivated	Wild	Garden	Notes
February	Thailand	Loei Province	roses		Phu Kadung National Park		scented
early February	Tanzania	Ngorogoro Crater	coffee trees	plantations			scented
mid-February	US	California/ Chico	almond trees	orchards			California Nut Festival; scented
February to April	Ecuador	throughout	orchids		lowlands & cloud forests		scented
February to April	Madeira	Funchal	freesias			city wide	scented
February to April	US	California/ San Marino	bulbs, South Africa (clivias, gladioli)			Huntington Botanical Garden	scented
February to April	US	South Carolina/ Charleston	azaleas			Middleton Place Plantation	scented
late February to early March	Costa Rica	Monteverde	bromeliads		Monteverde Cloud Forest Preserve		scented
late February to early March	Costa Rica	Monteverde	orchids, (1,200 species)		Monteverde Cloud Forest Preserve		scented
late February to early March	Japan	Chita City	plum trees		Sori Pond		Sori-iki Plum Blossom Festival (1,800 trees); scented

Bloom Time	Counry	Location	Flowers	Cultivated	Wild	Garden	Notes
late February to early April	Wales	South Pembrokeshire/ Tenby	daffodils, Tenby		old church yards		scented
March	Australia	Victoria/ Ballarat	begonias			Ballarat Botanical Garden	Begonia Festival
March	Israel	Mt. Gilboa	Gilboa iris		hillsides		scented
March	Mexico	San Miguel de Allende	jacaranda trees			city wide	scented
March	Portugal	Serra da Arrabida	daffodils, wild		shady hillsides		scented
March	US	California, Sierra Madre	wisteria			city park	Wisteria Festival "largest blooming plant in the world" (500' branches)
early March to early May	US	California/ Carlsbad	ranunculus	fields			Flower Fields
mid-March	Korea	Gwangyang/ Maehwa Village	apricot trees		hillsides		Apricot Festival; scented
late March	Japan	Takeda City, Saga	cherry trees			more than 2,500 sakura trees	Okajo Koen Cherry Blossom Festival; scented
mid-March to mid-May	US	California/ Death Valley	daisies, Panamint		valley floor		

Bloom Time	Counry	Location	Flowers	Cultivated	Wild	Garden	Notes
late March to April	Bermuda	throughout	lilies, Bermuda Easter			city wide	scented
late March to early April	Cypress	Karpaz Peninsula	anemones		hillsides		blooms amid ancient ruins; scented
late March to early April	Cypress	Karpaz Peninsula	orchids, bee		hillsides		scented
late March to early April	Turkey	Cappadocia	cherry trees		Goreme National Park		scented
late March to early April	US	Texas/ Austin	bluebonnets		open spaces	San Antonio Botanical Garden	scented
March to May (also year 'round)	England	throughout	gorse		roadsides, open woodlands		scented
March to May	India	Coorg	coffee trees	plantations			scented
March to May	Isles of Scilly	throughout	pansy, dwarf		coastal areas		scented
mid-March to mid-May	Madeira	Funchal	fuchsias, mimosa trees		along levadas		scented
March to June	England	Cornwall	blue quill		West Cornwall Coastal Path		
March to June	England	North Devon	daffodils		SW Coastal Path		scented

Bloom Time	Counry	Location	Flowers	Cultivated	Wild	Garden	Notes
April	Bhutan	Thimphu, Thumshing La National Park	orchids		upper cloud forest		scented
April	Bhutan	Thumshing La	daphne		upper cloud forest, Thumshing La National Park		scented
April	Bhutan	Chele Le La	iris		upper cloud forest		scented
April	Bhutan	Punakha	jacaranda trees			Punakha Dzong	scented
April	Canada	Quebec/ Grand-Metis	primulas			Reford Gardens	scented
April	Canary Islands	throughout	echiums		dry areas		
April	Caribbean	Dominica	Carib Wood trees		dry, coastal areas		
April	China	Beijing	crabapple trees			Temple of Heaven	scented
April	China	Beijing	wisteria			Hongluo Temple	scented
April	China	Guizhou/ Qianxi, Dafang	azaleas		natural azalea forest		Azalea Festival at Jinpo Village in Qianxi; scented
April	China	Nanjing	crabapple trees			Mochouhu Park	Flowering Crabapple Festival; scented

Bloom Time	Counry	Location	Flowers	Cultivated	Wild	Garden	Notes
April	China	Nanjing	rhododendron		Damingshan Mtn		Rhododendron Festival; scented
April	Greece	Crete	iris		hillsides		scented
April	Greece	Crete	thistle, Syrian		open spaces		
April	France	Paris	lilacs			city wide	scented
April	Jordan	Madaba	gladiola, wild		hillsides		scented
April	Jordan	Madaba	iris, black		hillsides		scented
April	Madeira	Funchal	wisteria			city wide	scented
April	Oman	Dhofar/ Salalah	frankincense trees		rocky areas/ Wadi Qahshan		frankincense souq
April	Portugal	Algarve	pimpernel, blue; sea pinks (thrift)		Sagres Point		
April	US	Arizona/ Phoenix	jacaranda trees			city wide	scented
April	US	Arizona/ Tombstone	rose tree			arbor, Rose Tree Inn Museum	"oldest rose tree in the world," 8,000 sqft arbor); scented
April	US	California/ Lancaster	poppies, California		Antelope Valley Poppy Reserve		California Poppy Festival; scented

Bloom Time	Counry	Location	Flowers	Cultivated	Wild	Garden	Notes
April	US	California/ Sacramento	wildflowers		Mather Field		vernal pools: wildflowers in a unique ecosystem
early April	Japan	Kyoto/ Kita Ward	camellias			Jizoan Temple	scented
early April	Japan	Kyoto	cherry trees			Byodo-in Temple, Fushimi Momoyama Castle, Heian Jingu Shrine	scented
early April	Japan	Nara	cherry trees			Nara Park, Kofukuji Temple	scented
early April	Japan	Shimane/ Muika-ichi Town	violets			city wide	Violet Festival; scented
early April	Japan	Yabu-gun	magnolias			Koshoji Temple	scented
early to mid-April	Greece	Crete	tulips, wild (lavender color)		hillsides		scented
early to mid-April	US	North Carolina/ Wilmington	azaleas			Airlie Gardens, Orton Plantation	NC Azalea Festival; scented
mid-April	Japan	Yoshino Mountain	cherry trees, white			Kumano National Park	sequential bloom-ing of centuries-old trees; scented
mid-late April	Belgium	Ghent	daffodils, tulips			city wide	scented

Bloom Time	Counry	Location	Flowers	Cultivated	Wild	Garden	Notes
mid-late April	Holland	Amsterdam, Aalsmeer, Limmen	tulips, daffodils, hyacinths	fields		Keukenhof Exhibition, Hortus Bulborum	Floating Flower Market, Aalsmeer Flower Auction (year 'round)
mid-late April	US	Georgia/ Savannah	wisteria		covering trees	city wide	scented
late April	Belgium	Ghent	azaleas			city wide	scented
late April	US	North Carolina/ Fayetteville	dogwoods			city wide	Dogwood Festival & dogwood trail; scented
late April to early May	Japan	Tokyo	wisteria			Kameido Tenjin Shrine	100 plants on 15 trellises planted 320 years ago; scented
late April to mid-May	Greece	Crete	anchusa		open spaces		
late April to mid-May	Greece	Crete	peonies, Cretan		open spaces		scented
late April to June	Peru	Machu Picchu, Aguas Calientes	orchids		along Inca Trail & at Machu Picchu		scented
April to May	Bermuda	throughout	Bermudiana		rocky areas, trails		

Bloom Time	Counry	Location	Flowers	Cultivated	Wild	Garden	Notes
April to May	Bhutan	Dochula Pass	magnolias, rhododendron		middle cloud forest		scented
April to May	Channel Isles	Jersey	foxgloves		coastal clifftops		scented
April to May	China	Suzhou	wisteria			Garden of the Humble Administrator	scented
April to May	Costa Rica	throughout	coffee trees	plantations			scented
April to May	Greece	Skopelos	freesias		fields		scented
April to May	Greece	Crete, Peleponnese	cyclamen, daphne, orchids		rocky outcrops		scented
April to May	Greece	throughout	anemones		rocky areas		scented
April to May	Morocco	Essaouira	argan trees		valleys		goats climb into trees to eat leaves when in bloom
April to May	Scotland	Harris Isle	orchids		hillsides		scented
April to May	Spain	Sevilla	orange trees			city wide, plazas	scented
April to May	Sweden	Lake Malaren	primulas		meadows		scented
April to mid-May	US	California/ Ft. Bragg	rhododendron			Mendocino Coast Botanic Garden	scented
April to June	Channel Isles	Guernsey	wild orchids	fields			scented

Bloom Time	Counry	Location	Flowers	Cultivated	Wild	Garden	Notes
April to June	Madeira	Funchal	proteas			gardens	
April to June	Malta	throughout	poppies		open spaces		scented
April to June	Spain	Alhambra	roses			gardens	scented
April to early July	Malaysia	Sabah	orchids		Mt. Kinabula National Park		scented
April to July	Bermuda	throughout	oleander, (Nerium)		hedges		scented
May	China	Hangzhou/ West Lake	peach trees			gardens	scented
May	Corsica	throughout	violets		alpine areas		scented
May	England	London/ Richmond Park	rhododendron			Isabella Plantation	scented
May	England	North Devon	bluebells		SW Coastal Path		scented
May	England	Surrey	bluebells		woodlands		scented
May	Greece	Crete	ebony		hillsides		
May	Japan	Hiroshima/ Fukuyama	roses			city wide	City of Roses, Rose Festival; scented
May	Japan	Nara/ Tenri City	azaleas			Chogakuji Temple	scented

Bloom Time	Counry	Location	Flowers	Cultivated	Wild	Garden	Notes
May	Norway	Hardangerfjord	apple, pear, cherry, plum trees	orchards			scented
May	Turkey	Miletus	poppies: purple, red, white		meadows		scented
May	US	Hawaii	jacaranda trees			city wide	scented
May	US	Colorado/ Dolores Canyon	phlox		foothills, canyons		scented
early May	Sardinia	Fonni	peonies, wild		hillsides		scented
early to mid-May	Canada	Ottawa	tulips			city wide	scented
early to| mid-May	Corsica	Evisa	mint, Corsican		shaded areas, Forest of Aitone		scented
early to mid-May	Corsica	Venaco	crocus, Corsican		upland valleys		scented
early to mid-May	Madeira	throughout	violets		alpine areas		scented
mid-May	Corsica	Evisa/ Spelunca Gorge	cyclamen		shaded areas		scented
mid-May	France	The Brenne, between Chatellerault & Chateauroux	orchids		meadows, Cherine Natural Reserve		scented

Bloom Time	Counry	Location	Flowers	Cultivated	Wild	Garden	Notes
mid-May	France	Grasse	peonies			estate gardens	scented
mid-May	Japan	Osaka/ Ikeda City	peonies			Kyuanji Temple	scented
mid-May	US	Arizona/ Tucson	saguaro cactus		hillsides, open spaces, Saguaro National Park	city wide	scented
mid-May	US	Michigan/ Holland	tulips	fields			Holland Tulip Festival; scented
mid-May	US	New York/ Rochester	lilacs			Highland Park	Lilac Festival; scented
mid-May	US	Rhode Island/ Kingston	crabapple trees	orchard/ University of Rhode Island			East Farm Crabapple Festival; scented
mid-May	Italy	Tuscany, Umbria	poppies, red		open spaces		scented
mid- to late May	England	Lake District	heather		open spaces	estate gardens	scented
mid- to late May	France	Giverny	wisteria, water lilies			Monet's Garden	scented
mid- to late May	Japan	Hokkaido	tulips	fields			Kamiyubetsu Tulip Park Fair (1 million bulbs); scented

Bloom Time	Counry	Location	Flowers	Cultivated	Wild	Garden	Notes
mid-May to early June	US	Oregon/ Salem	iris	fields		Schreiner's Iris Gardens	scented
mid-May to June	US	Florida/ Miami	Royal Poinciana trees (flame trees)			city wide	Royal Poinciana Festival; scented
late May	China	Shangdong/ Yantai	roses			city wide	Laizhou Rose Festival; scented
late May	England	Hever Castle	wisteria			estate gardens	scented
late May	France	Dordogne/ Castaing	fumana		meadows		
late May	France	Dordogne/ Castaing	globularia		meadows		
late May	France	Dordogne/ Castaing	meadow clary		meadows		
late May	Japan	Shimane/ Goka Village	rhododendron			Murakamiki Oki Rhododendron Park	scented
late May to early June	Bulgaria	Kazanlak	roses	fields in the Valley of Roses			Festival of Roses, one of largest producers of rose oil; scented

Bloom Time	Counry	Location	Flowers	Cultivated	Wild	Garden	Notes
late May to early June	Canada	British Columbia	violets		alpine areas		scented
late May to early June	Turkey	Manisa	tulips		Mt. Spil National Park		site of original tulips; scented
late May to early June	Turkey	Western & Central areas	daisies		meadows		
late May to early June	England	Wisely	azaleas			estate gardens	scented
late May to late June	US	Alaska	lousewort, wooly		rocky areas, tundra		
late May to late June	US	California/ Sierra Mtns	dogwoods		Sequoia & Kings Canyon National Park		among giant Sequoia trees; scented
late May to early July	Bhutan	Paro, Thimphu	poppies, blue		hillsides		scented
late May to July	Mongolia	Northern	geranium, cranesbill		meadows		scented
late May to October	US	Missouri/ Ozarks	coneflower, purple	fields			medicinal

Bloom Time	Counry	Location	Flowers	Cultivated	Wild	Garden	Notes
late May to early July	Turkey	Taurus Mtns/ Isparta	roses	fields			Carpet & Rose Festival (July), one of largest producers of rose oil; scented
late May to August	US	Alaska	forget-me-nots		meadows		scented
May to early June	Corsica	throughout	lavender, wild		hillsides		scented
May to early June	Greece	Crete, Cephalonia, Paxos	lavender, wild		open spaces		scented
May to June	Canada	Nova Scotia	rhododendron		rocky areas		scented
May to June	Canada	Nova Scotia	roses, wild		open spaces		scented
May to June	Canada	Nova Scotia	violets		bogs		scented
May to June	Greece	Crete	hibiscus			gardens	scented
May to June	India	Yumthang	alpine flowers, rhododendron		valley, Singhba Rhododendron Sanctuary		scented
May to June	Madeira	Funchal	lilies, Madonna			city wide	scented
May to June	Madeira	Funchal	orchids		hillsides	gardens	scented
May to June	Morocco	Kelaa, Dades Valley	roses	fields			Rose Festival; scented

Bloom Time	Counry	Location	Flowers	Cultivated	Wild	Garden	Notes
May to June	Sicily	coastal areas	geranium, scented (Pelargonium)		open spaces		scented
May to June	Spain	Camino de Santiago	wild herbs (lavender, rosemary, thyme) & wild roses		hillsides & along trail		scented
May to June	US	Mississippi/ Natchez	magnolias			city wide	scented
May to June	US	Montana	lilies, yellow glacier		low valleys, east side of Glacier National Park		scented
May to July	Canada	British Columbia/ Victoria	geranium, cranesbill			gardens	scented
May to August	Greece	Crete	wild herbs (oregano, rosemary, sage, thyme)		hillsides		scented
May to August	Nepal	Eastern	poppies, blue		hillsides		scented
May to August	US	Colorado	columbines		mountains, foothills	gardens	scented
May to October	Caribbean	throughout	frangipani (Plumeria)			common tree	scented

Bloom Time	Counry	Location	Flowers	Cultivated	Wild	Garden	Notes
May to October	India	Sikkim	primulas, magnolias, rhododendron poppies, blue		hillsides		60' tall rhodendron trees:scented
May to October	US	Hawaii	frangipani (Plumeria)		lowlands	city wide	used in leis; scented
May to November	Galapagos	Isabella Island	Darwin's cotton		dry zone		
May to November	Galapagos	Plazas Island	portulaca		coastal areas		scented
May to November	Galapagos	Santa Cruz Island	daisy trees (Scalesia)		humid highlands		
June	Channel Isles	Sark	bluebells		coastal clifftops		scented
June	Croatia	Hvar Island	lavender	fields			scented
June	Egypt	Cairo	jasmine, night-blooming			Mena House	scented
June	Egypt	Cairo	Royal Poinciana trees (flame trees)			city-wide	scented
June	Fiji	throughout	orchids		throughout		scented
June	France	Florac	orchid, monkey		Cevennes National park		scented

Bloom Time	Counry	Location	Flowers	Cultivated	Wild	Garden	Notes
June	France	Florac	rock rose		Cevennes National park		scented
June	Greece	throughout	chamomile, jasmine		open spaces	gardens	scented
June	Iceland	throughout	cotton grass		wet areas		
June	Iceland	throughout	violets		open spaces		scented
June	Japan	Gamagori City	hydrangeas			Katahara Hot Springs	Hydrangea Festival; scented
June	Japan	Toyohashi City/ Kamo cho	iris			Kamo Nurseries estate/ Kamo Shrine	1,500 varieties, 39,000 in bloom; Iris Festival; scented
June	Slovakia	Carpathian Mtns	columbines		Low Tatras National Park		scented
June	Slovakia	Carpathian Mtns	daphne		High Tatras National Park		scented
June	Slovakia	Carpathian Mtns	iris, Siberian		steppes, Slovak Raj National Park		scented
June	Slovakia	Muran Plateau	orchids		Muranska National Park		scented
June	Spain	Ordesa	butterworts		Ordesa National Park		

Bloom Time	Counry	Location	Flowers	Cultivated	Wild	Garden	Notes
June	Spain	Ordesa	pansy, horned		Ordesa National Park		scented
June	Spain	Picos de Europa	columbines		Fuente De		scented
June	Spain	Picos de Europa	heather		hillsides		scented
June	Spain	Picos de Europa	orchids		meadows		scented
June	Spain	Picos de Europa	pasqueflowers		meadows		
June	Spain	Picos de Europa	sea holly		rocky areas		
June	US	Michigan/ Mackinac Island	lilacs			gardens	Lilac Festival; scented
June	US	Oregon/ Portland	roses			city wide, parks	City of Roses, Rose Festival; scented
June	Wales	Shell Island	sea pink (thrift)		banks of estuary		scented
June	Spain	Picos de Europa	sea holly		rocky areas		
June	US	Michigan/ Mackinac Island				gardens	Lilac Festival; scented
June	US	Oregon/ Portland	roses			city wide, parks	City of Roses, Rose Festival; scented
June	Wales	Shell Island	sea pink (thrift)		banks of estuary		scented

Bloom Time	Counry	Location	Flowers	Cultivated	Wild	Garden	Notes
early June	England	Cotswolds	laburnum			Barnesley House	laburnum arch; scented
early June	Wales	North Wales	laburnum			Bodnant Gardens	laburnum arch; scented
early to mid-June	Denmark	Copenhagen	tulips			Tivoli Gardens	scented
early to mid-June	Greece	Pindos	foxgloves		Vikos Gorge		scented
early to mid-June	Greece	Pindos	orchids		Vikos Gorge		scented
early to mid-June	Greece	Pindos	ramondia		Vikos Gorge		scented
early to mid-June	Sweden	Oland	orchids		Schaferi Meadows		scented
mid-June	France	Pyrenees	gentian		high meadows, Pyrenees National Park		scented
mid-June	US	North Carolina/ Bakersville	rhododendron, wild		Roan Mtn		Rhododendron Festival; scented
late June	Bulgaria	Bansko	alpine wildflowers		mountain meadows, Pirin Mtns National Park		

Bloom Time	Counry	Location	Flowers	Cultivated	Wild	Garden	Notes
June to July	Iceland	throughout	bluebells		open spaces		scented
June to July	France	Pyrenees	daisies		meadows, Pyrenees National Park		scented site of original Shasta Daisy
June to July	France	Pyrenees	alpen rose (rhododendron)		meadows, Pyrenees National Park		scented
June to July	France	Pyrenees	iris, Pyrenean		meadows, Pyrenees National Park		scented
June to July	France	Pyrenees	ramondia		meadows, Pyrenees National Park		
June to July	France	Pyrenees	rock rose, Pyrenean		meadows, Pyrenees National Park		scented
June to July	Ireland	Burren	geranium, cranesbill		throughout		scented
June to July	Italy	Piedmont/ Asti	basil	fields			scented
June to July	Jordan	Petra	oleander, wild		wadis		scented
June to July	US	Missouri/ St. Louis	caperbush			Missouri Botanical Garden	scented
mid-June to mid-July	Channel Isles	Jersey	lavender	fields			scented

Bloom Time	Counry	Location	Flowers	Cultivated	Wild	Garden	Notes
mid-June to mid-July	US	Alaska, SE & SCentral	lilies, chocolate		coastal meadows		
mid- late June	France	Provence	lavender	fields			scented
late June to early July	England	Norfolk	lavender	fields			scented
late June to early July	Estonia	Osmussaar Island	orchids		meadows		scented
late June to July	England	Hertfordshire/ St. Albans	roses			Gardens of the Rose	scented
late June to early July	Austria	Austrian Tyrol/ Seefeld	alpine wildflowers		mountain meadows		
late June to mid-July	Estonia	Saaremaa	wildflowers		Tuhu Bog, Puhtu Forest, Laelatu Meadows		scented
late June to August|	Japan	Kyoto	lotus			Hokogoin Temple	scented
late June to August	US	Washington/ Sequim	lavender	fields			Sequim Lavender Festival; scented
June to August	Azores	throughout	sea lavender		coastal clifftops		
June to August	Canada	Yukon	fireweed		open spaces		Territorial Flower

Bloom Time	Counry	Location	Flowers	Cultivated	Wild	Garden	Notes
June to August	Canada	Yukon	heather, arctic		open spaces		burned as heating fuel (high resin content)
June to August	China	Kunming	lotus			Beijing Summer Palace	Garden of Harmonious Interest; scented
June to August	Denmark	Odense	fuchsias			Egeskov Castle, Kvaerndrup	scented
June to August	England	Isle of Wight	rock samphire		coastal clifftops		scented
June to August	Iceland	throughout	lupines		open spaces		scented
June to August	Iceland	throughout	primulas		open spaces	gardens	scented
June to August	Malta	throughout	sea lavender		coastal clifftops		
June to August	US	Colorado/ Vail	alpine wildflowers		mountain meadows	Betty Ford Alpine Gardens	world's highest botanical garden (8,200')
June to August	US	Montana/ Blackfeet Hwy	Indian paintbrush		meadows		
June to late August	Italy	Alta Badia	daphne		Dolomites		scented

Bloom Time	Counry	Location	Flowers	Cultivated	Wild	Garden	Notes
June to late August	Italy	Alta Badia	lilies, Turk's Cap		Dolomites		
June to late August	Italy	Alta Badia	morning glory		Dolomites		scented
June to late August	Italy	Alta Badia	rhododendron		Dolomites		scented
June to September	Scotland	Isle of Iona	fuchsias		hedges		scented
June to September	US	Texas	bluebells		open spaces		scented
June to October	Madeira	throughout	frangipani (Plumeria)		lowlands	city wide	scented
July	Canada	British Columbia/ Golden	edelweiss	fields			extract used in skin care products
July	Channel Isles	Jersey	orchids		meadows, marshes		scented
July	Iceland	throughout	poppies: Iceland, arctic		open spaces		scented
July	Scotland	throughout	bluebells		open spaces		scented
July	Slovenia	Julian Alps/ Ukanc	alpine wildflowers		mountain meadows		

Bloom Time	Counry	Location	Flowers	Cultivated	Wild	Garden	Notes
July	Switzerland	Swiss Alps/ Upper Engadine Valley	alpine wildflowers		mountain meadows		
early July	Japan	Tokyo/ Iriya	morning glory			Kishibojin Shrine	Morning Glory Festival & Market; scented
mid-to late July	Norway	Golsfjellet	alpine wildflowers		mountain meadows		
mid-to late July	Norway	Golsfjellet	orchids		bogs		scented
July to August	Canada	Nova Scotia	lilies,water		lakes, ponds		scented
July to August	China	Hangzhou/ West Lake	lotus			lakes	Lotus Festival; scented
July to August	Iceland	throughout	heather, arctic		open spaces		heather oil used in local spas
July to August	Japan	Hokkaido/ Furano	lavender	fields			scented
July to August	Nepal	Western	poppies, blue		alpine areas		scented
July to August	US	Wyoming	lupines		meadows, Grand Teton National Park		scented
July to September	South Africa	Namaqualand	daisies		Skilpad Reserve		

Bloom Time	Counry	Location	Flowers	Cultivated	Wild	Garden	Notes
July to January	Australia	New South Wales	geranium, scented (Pelargonium)			gardens	scented
weekend of August 15th even years	Belgium	Brussels	begonias				Floral Carpet at Grand- Place (700,000+ flowers used)
August	Bhutan	high country	alpine wildflowers, edelweiss		mountain meadows		
August	France	Arles	sunflowers	fields			
August	US	Kansas/ Goodland	sunflowers	fields			State Flower
mid-August to early September	Scotland	throughout	heather		hillsides, moors		National Heather Centre, Cher-rybank, Perth; scented
August to September	England	Devon, Yorkshire	heather		open spaces		scented
August to September	Scotland	lowlands	thistle, Scotch		open spaces		National Flower
August to September	South Africa	Namaqualand	wildflowers			Skilpad Reserve	scented

Bloom Time	Counry	Location	Flowers	Cultivated	Wild	Garden	Notes
August to September	US	Oregon/ Canby	dahlias	fields			Swan Island Dahlia Festival
August to October	Australia	SW, Albany/ Margaret River	wildflowers		open spaces		scented
August to October	US	Hawaii	ylang ylang trees		humid lowlands	gardens, parks	scented
August to October	Caribbean	throughout	ylang ylang trees		humid lowlands		scented
August to December	US	Hawaii/ Maui	silversword		Haleakala National Park		grows only inside this crater
September	Channel Isles	Jersey	autumn squill (Scilla)		coastal clifftops		scented
September	Ethiopia	Addis Ababa	daisies, Meskel		hillsides		
September	Greece	Crete	dittany of Crete		Imbros Gorge		scented
September	Madagascar	throughout	Fish Poison Tree (Barringtonia)		along shores		scented
September	Malaysia	Penang	orchids, giant		lowland rainforest	Burkit Jambul Orchid, Hibiscus, Reptile Gardens	scented
early September	Java	throughout	coffee trees	plantations			scented

Bloom Time	Counry	Location	Flowers	Cultivated	Wild	Garden	Notes
mid-September	England	Stoke-on-Trent	dahlias			Biddolph Grange Garden	
late September to early April	Isles of Scilly	throughout	narcissus	fields			scented
September to October	Australia	Brisbane	jacaranda trees			city wide	Goodna RSL Jacaranda Festival; scented
September to October	Australia	SW, Albany/ Margaret River	wildflowers & 70 species of orchid		open spaces		bloom progresses from Pilbara to Esper-ance
September to October	Channel Isles	Guernsey, Jersey	lilies, Guernsey, Jersey (Nerine)			gardens	Nerine Festival Guernsey; scented
September to October	China	Guilin, Hangzhou, Shanghai	osmanthus, sweet			city wide	Osmanthus Festi-vals; scented
September to October	Greece	Peleponnese	narcissus		rocky outcrops		scented
September to October	New Zealand	throughout	Kowhai tree		streamsides, forest edges, nature parks		

Bloom Time	Counry	Location	Flowers	Cultivated	Wild	Garden	Notes
September to October	New Zealand	Chatham Island	forget-me-nots, Chatham Island		coastal clifftops, Henga Scenic Reserve, Kangaroa Point		scented
September to October	South Africa	Pretoria	jacaranda trees			city wide	"Jacaranda City;" scented
September to November	Madeira	Funchal	lilies, belladonna, Guernsey or Jersey			city wide	scented
September to November	New Zealand	Alexandra	wildflowers		Pisa or Flat Top Hill Conservation Reserve		scented
September to December	India	Sikkim, Gangtok	orchids, 454 species			Orchidarium & Orchid Sanctuary	Flower Exhibition Center; scented
September to February	South Africa	Limpopo & Western Cape	geranium, scented (Pelargonium)		sheltered areas in mountains		scented
September to March	Tanzania	Tanga/ Usambara Mtns	African violets (Saintpaulia)		rainforest, Amani Nature Reserve		site of original African violets
October	Australia	Grampians	bauera & wildflowers		streamside		
early October	Tasmania	Wynyard	tulips	fields			Wynyard Tulip Festival; scented

Bloom Time	Counry	Location	Flowers	Cultivated	Wild	Garden	Notes
mid-October	Spain	Castilla la Mancha	crocus, saffron	fields			scented
late October	Iran	Khorasan Province	crocus, saffron	fields			scented
late October to early November	Australia	New South Wales/ Blackheath	rhododendron			Baccante Rhododendron Gardens	Blackheath Rhododendron Festival; scented
late October to early November	New Zealand	New Plymouth	rhododendron			city wide	Taranaki Rhododendron Festival; scented
late October to mid-November	New Zealand	Rotorua	azaleas, magnolias			city wide	scented
October to November	Greece	Peleponnese	crocus, purple		brushwood maquis		scented
October to February	Argentina	Calafate	calafate		slopes		edible fruit, wine
October to February	Madeira	Funchal	poinsettias			city wide	
October to February	US	Hawaii	proteas	fields		gardens	

Bloom Time	Counry	Location	Flowers	Cultivated	Wild	Garden	Notes
November	Argentina	Patagonia/ Ushuaia	orchids		high plateaus, Tierra del Fuego National Park		scented
November	Argentina	Patagonia/ Ushuaia	violet, yellow		high plateaus, Tierra del Fuego National Park		scented
November	Caribbean	Dominica/ Roseau Valley	jade vines		rainforest	gardens	scented
November	New Zealand	Auckland	roses			Parnell Gardens	Parnell Rose Fes-tival; scented
November to December	Argentina	Bariloche	fuchsia, wild		streamside		scented
November to December	Argentina	Bariloche	notro firebush		sandy areas, open spaces		
November to December	Argentina	Bariloche	rosa mosqueta		throughout		edible products made from hips; scented
November to February	Thailand	Lopburi, Saraburi	sunflower	fields			
November to March	Argentina	Bariloche/ Chalhuaco Valley	amancay (Alstroemeria)		open spaces		scented
November to April	Madeira	Funchal	camellias			Quinta do Palheiro Ferreiro	scented

Bloom Time	Counry	Location	Flowers	Cultivated	Wild	Garden	Notes
December	Caribbean	Bahamas	African tulip trees			throughout	
December	Mexico	Chiapas	bromeliads		cloud forest		
December	Mexico	Taxco	poinsettias		hillsides		site of original poinsettias
December	South Africa	southwestern Cape area	proteas	fields			
December	Tasmania	Scottsdale	lavender, poppies, pink opium	fields			scented
December to January	Madagascar	throughout	orchids, black			gardens	scented
December to mid-February	New Zealand	Otago	alpine wildflowers		hillsides		
December to March	Argentina	Calafate	sweet peas		open spaces, Glaciares National Park		scented
December to March	Argentina	Colon	petunias, wild		El Palmar National Park		site of original petunias; scented
December to March	Chile	between Valparaiso & Osorno	bellflower, Chilean		climbs trees in damp forests		National Flower
most of year	Brazil	Amazon River Basin	liles, giant Amazon		calm river inlets		scented

Bloom Time	Counry	Location	Flowers	Cultivated	Wild	Garden	Notes
most of year	Caribbean	Bahamas	bougainvillea			throughout	scented
most of year	China	Wulingyuan	wildflowers		open spaces		scented
most of year	Ecuador	Cayambe	roses	plantations			scented
most of year	Ecuador	foothills	bromeliads		cloud forest		
most of year	Egypt	Cairo	lotus, blue (Egyptian)			Egyptian Museum forecourt pool	scented
most of year (March to | May is best)	England	throughout	gorse		roadsides, open woodlands		scented
most of year	Greece	Crete	bougainvillea			city wide gardens	scented
most of year	Kenya	Nairobi area	bougainvillea			Karen Blixen House, Outspan Country Club, Mt. Kenya Safari Club	scented
most of year	India	South India	lotus			water gardens	National Flower; scented
most of year	Madagascar	Nosy Be	ylang ylang trees	plantations			scented

Bloom Time	Counry	Location	Flowers	Cultivated	Wild	Garden	Notes
most of year	Madeira	Funchal	azaleas, bougainvillea, hydrangea, jacaranda trees, fennel, wild lavender				scented
most of year	Malaysia	throughout	hibiscus		rainforest	gardens	National Flower; scented
most of year	Mexico	Tabasco	cacoa trees	groves			source of choco-late
most of year	Morocco	Atlas Mtns	lavender, wild		hillsides		scented
most of year	Philippines	throughout	jasmine		rainforest	gardens	National Flower; scented
most of year	Philippines	throughout	ylang ylang trees		humid lowlands	city wide	scented
most of year	Peru	Lima	bougainvillea			city wide	scented
most of year	Peru	Machu Picchu, Aguas Calientes	orchids		along Inca Trail & at Machu Picchu	hotel gardens	scented
most of year	Puerto Rico	throughout	hibiscus		rainforest	gardens	scented
most of year	US	Hawaii	bougainvillea			throughout	purple color; scented
most of year	US	Louisiana/ New Orleans	jasmine & night-blooming jasmine			city wide	scented

SECTION THREE

Flowers

Is Paris too far to go to smell lilacs in spring? Then try the Lilac Festival in Rochester, New York. Are you hooked on hydrangeas? Gamagori City in Japan celebrates this garden flower in June at the Katahara Hot Springs.

Flowers can enhance your trip in many ways. You might be visiting the Spanish Colonial city of San Miguel de Allende in Mexico and, pleasantly, the blooming jacaranda trees surrounding the buildings and throughout the plazas set the scene for you. Or you are in Tokyo in April and come across the Kameido Tenjin Shrine covered with 100 wisteria plants on 15 trellises that were planted 320 years ago. At either location, the perfumed air and the lavender-colored light from so many purple flowers will create an expanded memory of the scene.

You may never have thought that old, large and flowering plants can shape our memories of the places we visit. The camellias at two plantations near Charleston, South Carolina (Magnolia and Middleton Place) have the oldest camellias in the New World. Or consider the Tang Dynasty plum tree and the Ming Dynasty camellia at Black Dragon Pool in Longquan Hill, China. They are like living works of art, especially in February when they are in bloom.

Just as some bird tours focus on viewing a particular bird at a certain time in a specific location, single blossom plants exist that you might travel a great distance to see. These beauties include the bee orchid in its native Cypress; the blue, Egyptian lilies in Cairo; and the blue poppies in Bhutan. The proteas in South Africa, the silversword inside Maui's Haleakala Crater, and the saguaro blossoms in Arizona are also excellent reasons for this kind of botanical travel.

On the other hand, the beauty of mass plantings of flowers can take your breath away. These treasures include the field crops of lavender and roses grown worldwide for their essential oil; or the tulips, daffodils and hyacinths of Holland, Tasmania and Michigan. Bear in mind the fields of narcissus on the Isles of Scilly; saffron crocus in Spain and Iran; and pink, opium poppies in Tasmania. How about the fruit tree blossoms that are celebrated with festivals everywhere: almond trees in Northern California; apricot trees in Korea; and of course, the national spring pastime in Japan, hanami: cherry blossom viewing.

Many parts of the world offer spectacular displays of floral beauty. For example, the manicured "natural" gardens of the big estates in Europe, which are planted with azaleas and rhododendron for continuous bloom and visual impact. Or the expanse of one kind of flower that carpets an area for a limited time, such as the daisies in Namaqualand, South Africa; the bluebonnets of Texas; or the California poppies in the deserts east of Los Angeles and San Diego.

Almost every place on the planet has wildflowers, after all, they are the source of many of our garden plants and field crops. A meadow, hillside or other open space filled with a variety of wildflowers is a great memory of your trip; different colors, shapes and heights add another dimension to the natural landscape. The wildflowers of Corsica, Sweden, Mongolia, Israel, and Australia are startling in their incredible, but ephemeral beauty.

Wildflowers are not limited to summer in the temperate zones. Alpine flowers are also wildflowers that grow closer to the ground at the higher elevations around the world and can include what we call rock garden plants. Flowering plants such as the sea pinks of Portugal, rock samphire on the Isle of Wight, and the varieties of thyme growing throughout the Mediterranean bring color and interest to their native, harsh environments.

Marshes are another open space that provides a bounty of wildflowers. The marshes of Estonia and Jersey in the Channel Isles support orchids, lilies and primulas. Bogs in Iceland hold beautiful cotton grass while those in Norway feature a variety of orchids. And pastel-colored water lilies sprout year 'round in the lakes and ponds of Vietnam.

Coastal clifftops and dunes also provide a habitat for some of our favorite flowers. The sea lavender of the Azores, foxgloves of the Channel Isles, portulaca from the Galapagos, and the forget-me-nots of New Zealand are just a few examples of these now-common garden plants.

Some plants are grown for a specific product that overshadows their flowers: coffee trees in India bloom while the fruit is ripening and scent the air with a jasmine-like fragrance; arctic heather is harvested for its oil and used in spas; and the aroma from the fields of basil in the Piedmont area of Italy can be detected long before you see the plants. The appreciation of flowers is worldwide, which just expands the possibilities for *FLOWERtrippers.*

My *FLOWERtripping*™ Notes

Country	Location	Bloom Time	Flowers	Cultivated	Wild	Garden	Notes
African tulip trees	Caribbean	Bahamas	December			throughout	
Africanviolet (Saintpaulia)	Tanzania	Tanga/ Usambara Mtns	September to March		rainforest, Amani Nature Reserve		site of original African violets
almond trees	Portugal	Algarve	mid-January to February	orchards			scented
almond trees	US	California/ Chico	mid-February	orchards			California Nut Festival; scented
amancay (Alstroemeria)	Argentina	Bariloche/ Chalhuaco Valley	November to March			open spaces	scented
alpen rose (Rhododendron)	France	Pyrenees	June to July		lake shores, Pyrenees National Park		scented
alpine wildflowers	Austria	Austrian Tyrol/ Seefeld	late June to July		mountain meadows		
alpine wildflowers	Bhutan	high country	August		mountain meadows		
alpine wildflowers	Bulgaria	Bansko	late June		mountain meadows, Pirin Mtns National Park		

Country	Location	Bloom Time	Flowers	Cultivated	Wild	Garden	Notes
alpine wildflowers	India	Yumthang	May to June		valleys		
alpine wildflowers	New Zealand	Otago	December to mid-February		hillsides		
alpine wildflowers	Norway	Golsfjellet	mid- to late July		mountain meadows		
alpine wildflowers	Slovenia	Julian Alps/ Ukanc	July		mountain meadows		
alpine wildflowers	Switzerland	Swiss Alps/ Upper Engadine Valley	July		mountain meadows		
alpine wildflowers	US	Colorado/ Vail	June to August		mountain meadows	Betty Ford Alpine Gardens	world's highest botanical garden (8,200 ft.)
anchusa	Greece	Crete	late April to mid-May		open spaces		
anemones	Cyprus	Karpaz Peninsula	late March to early April		hillsides		blooms amid ancient ruins; scented
anemones	Greece	Crete	April		rocky outcrops		scented

Country	Location	Bloom Time	Flowers	Cultivated	Wild	Garden	Notes
apple, pear, plum, cherry trees	Norway	Hardangerfjord	May	orchards			scented
apricot trees	Korea	Gwangyang/ Maehwa Village	mid-March		hillsides		Apricot Festival; scented
argan trees	Morocco	Essaouira	April to May		valleys		goats climb into trees to eat leaves when in bloom
autumn squill (Scilla)	Channel Isles	Jersey	September		coastal clifftops		scented
azaleas	Belgium	Ghent	late April			city wide	scented
azaleas	China	Guizhou/ Qianxi, Dafang	April		natural azalea forest		Azalea Festival at Jinpo Village in Qianxi; scented
azaleas	Japan	Nara/Tenri City	May			Chogakuji Temple	scented
azaleas	Madeira	Funchal	most of year			city wide	scented
azaleas	New Zealand	Rotorua	late October to mid-November			city wide	scented
azaleas	England	Wisely	late May to early June			estate gardens	scented

Country	Location	Bloom Time	Flowers	Cultivated	Wild	Garden	Notes
azaleas	US	South Carolina/ Charleston	February to April			Middleton Place	scented
azaleas	US	North Carolina/ Wilmington	early to mid-April			Airlie Gardens, Orton Plantation	NC Azalea Festival; scented
basil	Italy	Piedmont/ Asti	June to July	fields			scented
bauera	Australia	Grampians	October		streamside		
begonias	Australia	Victoria/ Ballarat	March			Ballarat Botanical Gardens	Begonia Festival
begonias	Belgium	Brussels	weekend of August 15th even years				Floral Carpet at Grand-Place (700,000+ flowers used)
bellflower, Chilean	Chile	between Valparaiso & Osorno	December to March		climbs trees in damp forests		National Flower
Bermudiana	Bermuda	throughout	April to May		rocky areas, trails		
blue quill	England	Cornwall	March to June		West Coastal Path		
bluebells	Channel Isles	Sark	June		coastal clifftops		scented
bluebells	England	North Devon	May		SW Coastal Path		scented

Country	Location	Bloom Time	Flowers	Cultivated	Wild	Garden	Notes
bluebells	England	Surrey	May		woodlands		scented
bluebells	Iceland	throughout	June to July		open spaces		scented
bluebells	Scotland	throughout	July		open spaces		scented
bluebells	US	Texas	June to September		open spaces		scented
bluebonnets	US	Texas/ Austin	late March to early April		open spaces	San Antonio Botanical Garden	scented
bougainvillea	Caribbean	Bahamas	most of year			throughout	scented
bougainvillea	Greece	throughout	most of year			gardens	scented
bougainvillea	Kenya	Nairobi area	most of year			Karen Blixen House, Outspan Country Club, Mt. Kenya Safari Club	scented
bougainvillea	Madeira	Funchal	most of year			city wide, canopy over river running through city	scented
bougainvillea	Peru	Lima	most of year			city wide	scented
bougainvillea	US, Hawaii	throughout	most of year			throughout	scented
bromeliads	Costa Rica	Monteverde	late February to early March		Monteverde Cloud Forest		
bromeliads	Ecuador	foothills	most of year			cloud forest	

Country	Location	Bloom Time	Flowers	Cultivated	Wild	Garden	Notes
bromeliads	Mexico	Chiapas	December			cloud forest	
broom	Azores	throughout	March to May		open spaces		scented
bulbs, South Africa (clivias, gladioli)	US	California/ San Marino	February to April			Huntington Botanical Garden	scented
butterworts	Spain	Ordesa	June		Ordesa National Park		
cacao trees	Mexico	Tabasco	most of year	groves			source of chocolate
calafate	Argentina	Calafate	October to February		slopes		edible fruit, wine
camellias	China	Kunming	February			Golden Temple	camellia tree 500-800 years old; scented
camellias	Japan	Kyoto/ Kita Ward	early April			Jizoan Temple	scented
camellias	Madeira	Funchal	November to April			Quinta do Palheiro Ferreiro	scented
camellias	US	California/ Pasadena	January to February			Descanso Gardens	Camellia Festival; scented

Country	Location	Bloom Time	Flowers	Cultivated	Wild	Garden	Notes
camellias	US	South Carolina/ Charleston	March to April			Magnolia & Middleton Place Plantations	oldest camel-lias in the North America; scented
caperbush	US	Missouri/ St. Louis	June to July			Missouri Botanical Garden	
Carib Wood trees	Caribbean	Dominica	April		dry, coastal areas		
chamomile	Greece	throughout	June		open spaces		scented
cherry trees	Japan	Kyoto	early April			Byodo-in Temple, Fushimi Momoyama Castle, Heian Jingu Shrine	scented
cherry trees	Japan	Nara	early April			Nara Park, Kofukuji Temple	scented
cherry trees	Japan	Tokyo	late March to mid-April			estates, Ueno Oncho Park, Shinjuku Gyoen	scented
cherry trees	Japan	Takeda-city, Saga	late March			more than 2,500 sakura trees	Okajo Koen Cherry Blossom Festival; scented

Country	Location	Bloom Time	Flowers	Cultivated	Wild	Garden	Notes
cherry trees, white	Japan	Yoshino Mtn.	mid-April		Kumano National Park		sequential blooming of centuries-old trees; scented
cherry trees	Turkey	Cappadocia	late March to early April		Goreme National Park		scented
cherry trees	US	Washington, DC	late March to early April			Tidal Basin	National Cherry Blossom Festival; scented
coffee trees	Costa Rica	throughout	April to May	plantations			scented
coffee trees	India	Coorg	March to May	plantations			scented
coffee trees	Java	throughout	early September	plantations			scented
coffee trees	Tanzania	Ngorogoro Crater	early February	plantations			scented
columbine	Slovakia	Carpathian Mountains	June		Low Tatras National Park		scented
columbine	Spain	Picos de Europa	June		Fuente De		scented
columbine	US	Colorado	May to August		mountains, foothills	gardens	scented
coneflower, purple	US	Missouri/ Ozarks	late May to October	fields	meadows, prairies		medicinal
cotton grass	Iceland	throughout	June		wet areas		

Country	Location	Bloom Time	Flowers	Cultivated	Wild	Garden	Notes
crabapple trees	China	Beijing	April			Temple of Heaven	scented
crabapple trees	China	Nanjing	April			Mochouhu Park	Flowering Crabapple Festival; scented
crabapple trees	US	Rhode Island/ Kingston	mid-May	orchard/ University of Rhode Island			East Farm Crabapple Festival; scented
crocus, Corsican	Corsica	Venaco	early to mid-May		upland valleys		scented
crocus, purple	Greece	Peleponnese	October to November		brushwood macquis		scented
crocus, saffron	Spain	Castilla la Mancha	mid-October	fields			scented
crocus, saffron	Iran	Khorasan Province	late October	fields			scented
cyclamen	Corsica	Evisa/ Spelunca Gorge	early to mid-May		shaded areas		scented
cyclamen	Greece	Crete, Peleponnese	April to May		rocky outcrops		scented
daffodils	Belgium	Ghent	mid- to late April			city wide	Floriales (floral display held every 5 years. Next is 2010)

Country	Location	Bloom Time	Flowers	Cultivated	Wild	Garden	Notes
daffodils	Holland	Amsterdam, Aalsmeer, Limmen	mid- to late April	fields		Keukenhof Exhibition, Hortus Bulborum	Floating Flower Market, Aalsmeer Flower Auction (year 'round)
daffodils	England	North Devon	March to June		SW Coast Path		scented
daffodils, Tenby	Wales	South Pembrokeshire/ Tenby	late February to early April		old church yards		scented
daffodils, wild	Portugal	Serra da Arrabida	March		shady hillsides		scented
dahlias	England	Stoke-on-Trent	mid-September			Biddulph Grange Garden	
dahlias	US	Oregon/ Canby	August to September	fields			Swan Island Dahlia Festival
daisy trees (Scalesia)	Galapagos	Santa Cruz Island	May to November		humid highlands		
daisy, Meskel	Ethiopia	Addis Ababa	September		hillsides		
daisies	France	Pyrenees	June to July		meadows, Pyrenees National Park		site of original Shasta Daisy
daisies	South Africa	Namaqualand	July to September		Skilpad Reserve		
daisies	Turkey	Western & Central	late May to early June		open spaces		

Country	Location	Bloom Time	Flowers	Cultivated	Wild	Garden	Notes
daisies, Panamint	US	California/ Death Valley	mid-March to mid-May		valley floor		
daphne	Bhutan	Thumshing La	April		upper cloud forest in Thumshing La National Park		scented
daphne	Greece	Crete	April		rocky outcrops		scented
daphne	Italy	Alta Badia	June to late August		Dolomites		scented
daphne	Slovakia	Carpathian Mtns	June		High Tatras Mountains National Park		scented
Darwin's cotton	Galapagos	Isabella Island	May to November		dry zone		
dittany of Crete	Greece	Crete	September		Imbros Gorge		scented
dogwoods	US	California/ Sierra Mtns	late May to late June		Sequoia & Kings Canyon National Park		among giant Sequoia trees; scented
dogwoods	US	North Carolina/ Fayetteville	late April			city wide	Dogwood Festival & dogwood trail; scented

Country	Location	Bloom Time	Flowers	Cultivated	Wild	Garden	Notes
ebony	Greece	Crete	May		hillsides		
echiums	Canary Islands	throughout	April		dry areas		
echiums (Pride of Madeira)	Madeira	throughout	January to July		open spaces		
edelweiss	Bhutan	high country	August		meadows		
edelweiss	Canada	British Columbia/ Golden	July	fields			extract used in skin care products
fennel	Madeira	Funchal	most of year		hillsides		scented
fireweed	Canada	Yukon	June to August		open spaces		Territorial Flower
Fish Poison Tree (Barringtonia)	Madagascar	coastal areas	September		along shores		scented
forget-me-nots	US	Alaska	late May to August		meadows		State Flower; scented
forget-m-knots, Chatham Island	New Zealand	Chatham Islands	September to October		coastal clifftops, Henga Scenic Reserve, Kaingaroa Point		scented
foxgloves	Channel Isles	Jersey	April to May		coastal clifftops		scented
foxgloves	Greece	Pindos	early to mid-June		Vikos Gorge		

Country	Location	Bloom Time	Flowers	Cultivated	Wild	Garden	Notes
frangipani (Plumeria)	Caribbean	throughout	May to October			lowlands	scented
frangipani (Plumeria)	Madeira	throughout	June to October		lowlands	city wide	scented
frangipani (Plumeria)	US	Hawaii	May to October			lowlands	used in leis; scented
frankincense trees	Oman	Dhofar/ Salalah	April		rocky areas/ Wadi Qahshan		frankincense souq
freesias	Greece	Skopelos	April to May		fields		scented
freesias	Madeira	Funchal	February to April			city wide	scented
fuchsias, wild	Argentina	Bariloche	November to December		streamside		scented
fuchsias	Denmark	Odense	June to August			Egeskov Castle, Kvaerndrup	scented
fuchsias	Madeira	Funchal	mid-March to mid-May		along levadas		scented
fuchsias	Scotland	Isle of Iona	June to September		hedges		scented
fumana	France	Dordogne/ Castaing	late May		meadows		
gentian	France	Pyrenees	mid-June		high meadows, Pyrenees National Park		scented

Country	Location	Bloom Time	Flowers	Cultivated	Wild	Garden	Notes
geranium, cranesbill	Canada	British Columbia/ Victoria	May to July			gardens	scented
geranium, cranesbill	Ireland	Burren	June to early July		throughout		scented
geranium, cranesbill	Mongolia	Northern	May to July		meadows		scented
geranium, scented (Pelargonium)	Australia	New South Wales	July to January		gardens		scented
geranium, scented (Pelargonium)	Sicily	coastal areas	May to June		open spaces		scented
geranium, scented (Pelargonium)	South Africa	Limpopo & Western Cape	September to February		sheltered areas in mountains		scented
gladiola, wild	Jordan	Madaba	April		hillsides		scented
globularia	France	Dordogne/ Castaing	late May		meadows		
gorse	Corsica	throughout	March to April		hillsides		scented
gorse	England	throughout	most of year (March to May is best)		roadsides, open woodlands		scented

Country	Location	Bloom Time	Flowers	Cultivated	Wild	Garden	Notes
heather, arctic	Canada	Yukon	June to August		open spaces		burned as heating fuel (high resin content)
heather	England	Lake District	mid- to late May			estate gardens	scented
heather	England	Devon, Yorkshire	August to September		open spaces, moors		scented
heather, arctic	Iceland	throughout	July to August		open spaces		heather oil used in local spas
heather	Scotland	throughout	mid-August to early September		hillsides, moors		National Heather Centre, Cherrybank, Perth; scented
heather	Spain	Picos de Europa	June		hillsides		scented
hibiscus	Greece	Crete	May to June			gardens	scented
hibiscus	Malaysia	throughout	most of year		rainforest	gardens	National Flower; scented
hibiscus	Puerto Rico	throughout	most of year		rainforest	gardens	scented
hyacinths	Holland	Amsterdam, Aalsmeer, Limmen	mid- to late April	fields		Keukenhof Exhibition, Hortus Bulborum	Floating Flower Market, Aalsmeer Flower Auction (year 'round)

Country	Location	Bloom Time	Flowers	Cultivated	Wild	Garden	Notes
hydrangeas	Madeira	Funchal	most of year		lines the road to Encumeada Pass		scented
hydrangeas	Japan	Gamagori City	June			Katahara Hot Springs	Hydrangea Festival; scented
Indian paintbrush	US	Montana/ Blackfeet Hwy	June to August		meadows		
iris	Bhutan	Chele Le La	April		upper cloud forest		scented
iris	Greece	Crete	April		hillsides		scented
iris, Gilboa	Israel	Mt. Gilboa	March		hillsides		scented
iris, Japanese	Japan	Toyohashi City/ Kamo cho	June			Kamo Nurseries, estate/ Kamo Shrine	1,500 varieties, 39,000 in bloom, Iris Festival; scented
iris, black	Jordan	Madaba	April		hillsides		scented
iris, Pyrenean	France	Pyrenees	June to July		Pyrenees National Park		scented
iris, Siberian	Slovakia	Carpathian Mtns	June		steppes, Slovak Raj National Park		scented
iris	US	Oregon/ Salem	mid-May to early June	fields		Schreiner's Iris Gardens	scented

Country	Location	Bloom Time	Flowers	Cultivated	Wild	Garden	Notes
jacaranda trees	Australia	Brisbane	September to October			city wide	Goodna RSL Jacaranda Festival; scented
jacaranda trees	Bhutan	Punakha	April			Punakha Dzong	scented
jacaranda trees	Madeira	Funchal	most of year			city wide	scented
jacaranda trees	Mexico	San Miguel de Allende	March			city wide	scented
jacaranda trees	South Africa	Pretoria	September to October			city wide	"Jacaranda City;" scented
jacaranda trees	US	Arizona/ Phoenix	April			city wide	scented
jacaranda trees	US	Hawaii	May			city wide	scented
jade vines	Caribbean	Dominica/ Roseau Valley	November		rainforest	gardens	scented
jasmine, night-blooming	Greece	throughout lower elevations	June			gardens	scented
jasmine, night-blooming	Egypt	Cairo	June			Mena House	scented
jasmine	Philippines	throughout	most of year		rainforest	gardens	National Flower; scented
jasmine & night-blooming jasmine	US	Louisiana/ New Orleans	most of year			city wide	scented

Country	Location	Bloom Time	Flowers	Cultivated	Wild	Garden	Notes
Kowhai trees	New Zealand	throughout	September to October		streamside, forest edges, nature parks		
laburnum, wild	Corsica	lower elevations	March to April		throughout		scented
laburnum	England	Cotswolds	early June			Barnesley House	laburnum arch, scented
laburnum	Wales	North Wales	early June			Bodnant Gardens	laburnum arch, scented
lavender	Channel Isles	Jersey	mid-June to mid-July	fields			scented
lavender, wild	Corsica	throughout	May to early June		hillsides		scented
lavender	Croatia	Hvar Island	June	fields			scented
lavender	England	Norfolk	late June to July	fields			scented
lavender	France	Provence	mid- to late June	fields			scented
lavender, wild	Greece	Cephalonia, Paxos, Crete	May to early June		open spaces		scented
lavender	Japan	Hokkaido/ Furano	July to August	fields			scented
lavender, wild	Madeira	Funchal	most of year		hillsides		scented

Country	Location	Bloom Time	Flowers	Cultivated	Wild	Garden	Notes
lavender, wild	Morocco	Atlas Mtns.	most of year		hillsides		scented
lavender	New Zealand	Napier, Kaikoura, Waikato	January	fields			scented
lavender	Tasmania	Scottsdale	December	fields			scented
lavender	US	Washington/ Sequim	late June to August	fields			Sequim Lavender Festival; scented
lilacs	France	Paris	April			city wide	scented
lilacs	US	Michigan/ Mackinac Island	June			gardens	Lilac Festival; scented
lilacs	US	New York/ Rochester	mid-May			Highland Park	Lilac Festival; scented
lilies, arum	Madeira	Funchal	January to June			city wide	scented
lilies, belladonna	Madeira	Funchal	September to November			city wide	scented
lilies, Bermuda Easter	Bermuda	throughout	late March to April			gardens	scented
lilies, chocolate	US	Alaska, SE & SCentral	mid-June to mid-July		coastal meadows		
lilies, Madonna	Madeira	Funchal	May to June			city wide	scented

Country	Location	Bloom Time	Flowers	Cultivated	Wild	Garden	Notes
lilies, Guernsey, Jersey (Nerine)	Channel Isles	Guernsey, Jersey	September to October			gardens	Nerine Festival Guernsey; scented
lilies, Guernsey, Jersey	Madeira	Funchal	September to November			city wide	scented
lilies, giant Amazon	Brazil	Amazon River Basin	most of year		calm river water inlets		scented
lilies, Turk's Cap	Italy	Alta Badia	June to late August		Dolomites		
lilies, water	Canada	Nova Scotia	July to August		lakes, ponds		scented
lilies, yellow glacier	US	Montana	May to June		low valleys, east side of Glacier National Park		scented
lotus	China	Hangzhou/ West Lake	July to August			lakes	Lotus Festival; scented
lotus	China	Kunming Lake	June to August			Beijing Summer Palace	Garden of Harmonious Interest; scented
lotus, blue (Egyptian)	Egypt	Cairo	most of year			Egyptian Museum forecourt pool	scented
lotus	India	South India	most of year			water gardens	National Flower; scented

Country	Location	Bloom Time	Flowers	Cultivated	Wild	Garden	Notes
lotus	Japan	Kyoto	late June to August			Hokogoin Temple	scented
lotus	Vietnam	throughout	most of year		lakes & ponds		National Flower; scented
lousewort, wooly	US	Alaska	late May to late June		rocky areas, tundra		
lupines	Iceland	throughout	June to August		open spaces		scented
lupines	Peru	Urubamba Valley	January		open spaces		scented
lupines	US	Wyoming	July to August		meadows, Grand Teton National Park		scented
magnolias	India	Sikkim	May-October		hillsides		scented
magnolias	Bhutan	Dochula Pass	April to May		middle cloud forest		scented
magnolias	Japan	Yabu-gun	early April			Koshoji Temple	scented
magnolias	New Zealand	Rotorua	late October to mid-November			gardens	scented
magnolias	US	Mississippi/ Natchez	May to June			city wide	scented
meadow clary	France	Dordogne/ Castaing	late May		meadows		

Country	Location	Bloom Time	Flowers	Cultivated	Wild	Garden	Notes
mimosa trees	France	Mandelieu	February			city wide	Mimosa Festival; scented
mimosa trees	Madeira	Funchal	mid-March to mid-May		along levadas		scented
mint, Corsican	Corsica	Evisa	early to mid-May		shaded areas, Forest of Aitone		scented
morning glory	Italy	Alta Badia	June to late August		Dolomites		scented
morning glory	Japan	Tokyo/ Iriya	early July		Kishibojin Shrine		Morning Glory Festival & Market; scented
narcissus	Isles of Scilly	throughout	late September to early April	fields			scented
narcissus	Greece	Peleponnese	September to October		rocky outcrops		scented
notro firebush	Argentina	Bariloche	November to December		sandy areas open spaces		
oleander, (Nerium)	Bermuda	throughout	April to July			hedges	scented
oleander, (Nerium)	Jordan	Petra	June to July		wadis		scented
orange trees	Spain	Sevilla	April to May			city wide	scented

Country	Location	Bloom Time	Flowers	Cultivated	Wild	Garden	Notes
orchids	Argentina	Patagonia/ Ushuaia	November		high plateaus, Tierra del Fuego National Park		scented
orchids	Australia	SW, Albany/ Margaret River	September to October			throughout	scented
orchids	Bhutan	Thimphu, Thumshing La National Park	April		upper cloud forest		scented
orchids, wild	Channel Isles	Guernsey	April to June	fields			scented
orchids	Channel Isles	Jersey	July		meadows, marshes		scented
orchids, (1,200 species)	Costa Rica	Monteverde	late February to early March		Monteverde Cloud Forest		scented
orchids, bee	Cypress	Karpaz Peninsula	late March to April		hillsides		scented
orchids	Ecuador	throughout	February to April		lowlands & cloud forests		scented
orchids	Estonia	Osmussaar Island	late June to early July		meadows		scented
orchids	Fiji	throughout	June		shaded areas		scented
orchids	France	The Brenne, between Chatellerault & Chateauroux	mid-May		meadows, Cherine Natural Reserve		scented

Country	Location	Bloom Time	Flowers	Cultivated	Wild	Garden	Notes
orchids, monkey	France	Florac	June		Cevennes National Park		scented
orchids	Greece	Crete	April to May		hillsides		scented
orchids	Greece	Pindos	early to mid-June		Vikos Gorge		scented
orchids, 454 species	India	Sikkim, Gangtok	September to December			Orchidarium & Orchid Sanctuary	Flower Exhibition Center; scented
orchids, black	Madagascar	throughout	December to January			gardens	scented
orchids	Madeira	Funchal	May to June		hillsides	gardens	scented
orchids, giant	Malaysia	Penang	September		lowland rainforest	Bukit Jambul Orchid, Hibiscus, Reptile Gardens	scented
orchids	Malaysia	Sabah	April to early July		Mt. Kinabula National Park		scented
orchids	Norway	Golsfjellet	mid- to late July		bogs		scented
orchids	Peru	Machu Picchu, Aguas Calientes	most of year, late April to June is best		along Inca Trail & Machu Picchu	hotel gardens	scented
orchids	Scotland	Harris Isle	April to May		open spaces		scented
orchids	Slovakia	Muran Plateau	June		Muranska National Park		scented

Country	Location	Bloom Time	Flowers	Cultivated	Wild	Garden	Notes
orchids	Spain	Picos de Europa	June		meadows		scented
orchids	Sweden	Oland	early to mid-June		Schaferi Meadows		scented
osmanthus, sweet	China	Guilin, Hangzhou, Shanghai	September to October				Osmanthus Festivals; scented
pansy, dwarf	Isles of Scilly	throughout	March to May		coastal areas		scented
pansy, horned	Spain	Ordesa	June		Ordesa National Park		scented
pasqueflowers	Spain	Picos de Europa	June		meadows		scented
peach trees	China	Hangzhou/ West Lake	May			gardens	scented
peonies	China	Louyang	late April to mid-May			city wide	Peony Festival; scented
peonies	France	Grasse	mid-May			gardens	scented
peonies, Cretan	Greece	Crete	late April to mid-May		open spaces		scented
peonies	Japan	Osaka/ Ikeda City				Kyuanji Temple	scented

Country	Location	Bloom Time	Flowers	Cultivated	Wild	Garden	Notes
peonies	Sardinia	Fonni	early May		hillsides		scented
petunias, wild	Argentina	Colon	December to March		El Palmar National Park		site of original petunias; scented
phlox	US	Colorado/ Dolores Canyon	May		foothills, canyons		scented
pimpernel, blue	Portugal	Algarve	April		Sagres Point		
plum trees	Japan	Chita City	late February to early March			Sori Pond	Sori-iki Plum Blossom Festival (1,800 trees); scented
poinsettias	Madeira	Funchal	October to February			city wide	
poinsettias	Mexico	Taxco	December		hillsides		site of original poinsettias
poppies, blue	Bhutan	Paro, Thimphu	late May to July		hillsides		scented
poppies: Iceland, arctic	Iceland	throughout	July		open spaces		scented
poppies, blue	India	Sikkim	May to October		hillsides		scented
poppies, red	Italy	Tuscany, Umbria	mid-May		open spaces		scented

Country	Location	Bloom Time	Flowers	Cultivated	Wild	Garden	Notes
poppies	Malta	throughout	April to June		open spaces		scented
poppies, blue	Nepal	Western	July to August		alpine areas		scented
poppies, blue	Nepal	Eastern	May to August		hillsides		scented
poppies, pink opium	Tasmania	Scottsdale	December	fields			scented
poppies: purple, red, white	Turkey	Miletus	May		meadows		scented
poppies, California	US	California/ Lancaster	April		Antelope Valley Poppy Reserve		California Poppy Festival
portulaca	Galapagos Islands	Plazas Island	May to November		coastal areas		scented
primulas	Canada	Quebec/ Grand-Metis	April			Reford Gardens	scented
primulas	Iceland	throughout	June to August		open spaces	gardens	scented
primulas	India	Sikkim	May to October		hillsides		scented
primulas	Sweden	Lake Malaren	April to May		meadows		scented
proteas	Madeira	Funchal	April to June			gardens	

Country	Location	Bloom Time	Flowers	Cultivated	Wild	Garden	Notes
proteas	South Africa	southwestern Cape area	December	fields			
proteas	US	Hawaii	October to February	fields		gardens	
ramondia	France	Pyrenees	June to July		shady boulders, Pyrenees National Park		
ramondia	Greece	Pindos	early to mid-June		Vikos Gorge		
ranunculus	US	California/ Carlsbad	early March to early May	fields			Flower Fields
rhododendron	Australia	New SouthWales/ Blackheath	late October to early November			Baccante Rhododendron Gardens	Blackheath Rhododendron Festival; scented
rhododendron	Bhutan	Dochula Pass	April to May		middle cloud forest		scented
rhododendron	Canada	Nova Scotia	May to June		rocky areas		scented
rhododendron	China	Nanning	April		Damingshan Mtn.		Rhododendron Festival; scented
rhododendron	England	London/ Richmond Park	May			Isabella Plantation	scented

Country	Location	Bloom Time	Flowers	Cultivated	Wild	Garden	Notes
rhododendron	India	Sikkim	May to October		hillsides		60′ tall rhododendron trees; scented
rhododendron	India	Yumthang	May to June		valley, Singbha Rhododendron Sanctuary		scented
rhododendron	Italy	Alta Badia	June to late August		Dolomites		scented
rhododendron	Japan	Shimane/ Goka Village	late May			Murakamiki Oki Rhododendron Park	scented
rhododendron	New Zealand	New Plymouth	late October to early November			city wide	Taranaki Rhododendron Festival; scented
rhododendron	US	California/ Ft. Bragg	April to mid-May			Mendocino Coast Botanic Garden	scented
rhododendron	US	North Carolina/ Bakersville	mid-June		Roan Mtn		Rhododendron Festival; scented
rock roses	France	Florac	June		Cevennes National Park		scented
rock roses, Pyrenean	France	Pyrenees	June to July		Pyrenees National Park		scented
rock samphire	England	Isle of Wight	June to August		coastal clifftops		scented

Country	Location	Bloom Time	Flowers	Cultivated	Wild	Garden	Notes
rosa mosqueta	Argentina	Bariloche	November to December		throughout		edible products made from hips; scented
rose tree	US	Arizona/ Tombstone	April			arbor, Rose Tree Inn Museum	"oldest rose tree in the world" (8,000 sqft arbor); scented
roses	Bulgaria	Kazanlak	late May to early June	fields in Valley of Roses			Festival of Roses, one of largest producers of rose oil; scented
roses, wild	Canada	Nova Scotia	May to June		open spaces		scented
roses	China	Shandong/ Yantai	late May			city wide	Laizhou Rose Festival; scented
roses	Ecuador	Cayambe	most of year	plantations			scented
roses	England	Hertfordshire/ St. Albans	late June to July			Gardens of the Rose	scented
roses	Japan	Hiroshima/ Fukuyama	May			city wide	City of Roses, Rose Festival; scented

Country	Location	Bloom Time	Flowers	Cultivated	Wild	Garden	Notes
roses	Morocco	Kelaa/ Dades Valley	May to June	fields			Rose Festival; scented
roses	New Zealand	Auckland	November			Parnell Gardens	Parnell Rose Festival; scented
roses	Spain	Alhambra	April to June			gardens	scented
roses, wild	Spain	Camino de Santiago	May to June		hillsides & along trail		scented
roses	Thailand	Loei Province	February		Phu Kradung National Park		scented
roses	Turkey	Taurus Mtns/ Isparta	late May to early July	fields			Carpet & Rose Festival (July), one of largest producers of rose oil; scented
roses	US	Oregon/ Portland	June			city wide, parks	City of Roses, Rose Festival; scented
Royal Poinciana trees (flame trees)	Egypt	Cairo	June			city wide	scented
Royal Poinciana trees (flame trees)	US	Florida/ Miami	mid-May to June			city wide	Royal Poinciana Festival; scented

Country	Location	Bloom Time	Flowers	Cultivated	Wild	Garden	Notes
saguaro	US	Arizona/ Tucson	May		hillsides, open spaces, Saguaro National Park	city wide	scented
sea holly	Spain	Picos de Europa	June		rocky areas		
sea lavender	Azores	throughout	June to August		coastal clifftops		
sea lavender	Malta	throughout	June to August		coastal clifftops		
sea pinks, (thrift)	Portugal	Algarve/ Monchique	April		Sagres Point		
sea pinks, (thrift)	Wales	Shell Island	June		banks of estuary		scented
silversword	US	Hawaii/ Maui	August to December		Haleakala National Park		grows only inside this crater
sunflowers	France	Arles	August	fields			
sunflowers	Thailand	Lopburi, Saraburi	November to February	fields			
sunflowers	US	Kansas/ Goodland	August	fields			State Flower
sweet peas	Argentina	Calafate	December to March		open spaces, Glaciares National Park		scented

Country	Location	Bloom Time	Flowers	Cultivated	Wild	Garden	Notes
thistle, Scotch	Scotland	lowlands	August to September		open spaces		National Flower
thistle, Syrian	Greece	Crete	April		open spaces		
tissue flowers	Kenya	Masai Mara	January		open spaces		
tulips	Belgium	Ghent	mid- to late April			city wide	Floriales (floral display held every 5 years. Next is 2010)
tulips	Canada	Ottawa	early to mid-May			city wide	scented
tulips	Denmark	Copenhagen	mid- to early June			Tivoli Gardens	scented
tulips, wild (lavender color)	Greece	Crete	early to mid-April		hillsides		scented
tulips	Holland	Amsterdam, Aalsmeer, Limmen	mid- to late April	fields		Keukenhof Exhibition, Hortus Bulborum	Floating Flower Market, Flower Auction year 'round
tulips	Japan	Hokkaido	mid- to late May	fields			Kamiyubetsu Tulip Park Fair (1million bulbs
tulips	Tasmania	Wynyard	early October	fields			Wynyard Tulip Festival; scented

Country	Location	Bloom Time	Flowers	Cultivated	Wild	Garden	Notes
tulips	Turkey	Manisa	late May to early June		Mt. Spil National Park		site of original tulips; scented
tulips	US	Michigan/ Holland	mid-May	fields			Holland Tulip Festival; scented
violets, yellow	Argentina	Patagonia/ Ushuaia	November		high plateaus, Tierra del Fuego National Park		scented
violets	Canada	British Columbia	late May to early June		alpine areas		scented
violets	Canada	Nova Scotia	May to June		bogs		scented
violets	Corsica	throughout	May		alpine areas		scented
violets	Iceland	throughout	June		open spaces		scented
violets	France	Toulouse	February			city wide	Violet Festival; scented
violets	Japan	Shimane/ Muikaichi Town	early April			city wide	Violet Festival; scented
violets	Madeira	Funchal	early to mid-May		alpine areas		scented
violets	Spain	Camino de Santiago	April to May		hillsides		scented
wildflowers	Australia	Grampians	October		throughout		scented

Country	Location	Bloom Time	Flowers	Cultivated	Wild	Garden	Notes
wildflowers	Australia	SW, Albany/ Margaret River	August to October		open spaces		bloom progresses from Pilbara to Esperance
wildflowers	China	Wulingyuan	most of year		open spaces		scented
wildflowers	Estonia	Saaremaa	late June to mid-July		Tuhu Bog, Puhtu Forest, Laelatu Meadows		scented
wildflowers	Israel	Galilee	February		Atzmon Mtn to Yodfat Ridge		scented
wildflowers	New Zealand	Alexandra	September to November		Pisa or Flat Top Hill Conservation Reserve		scented
wildflowers	South Africa	Namaqualand	August to September		Skilpad Reserve		scented
wildflowers	US	California/ Sacramento	April		Mather Field		vernal pools: wildflowers in a unique ecosystem
wild herbs (oregano, rosemary, thyme, sage)	Greece	Crete	May to August		hillsides		scented

Country	Location	Bloom Time	Flowers	Cultivated	Wild	Garden	Notes
wild herb (lavender, rosemary, thyme)	Spain	Camino de Santiago	May to June		hillsides & along trail		scented
wisteria	China	Beijing	April			Hongluo Temple	scented
wisteria	China	Suzhou	April			Humble Administrator's Garden	scented
wisteria	England	Kent	late May			Hever Castle	scented
wisteria	France	Giverny	mid- to late May			Monet's Garden	scented
wisteria	Japan	Tokyo	late April to early May			Kameido Tenjin Shrine	100 plants on 15 trellises planted 320 years ago; scented
wisteria	Madeira	Funchal	April			city wide	scented
wisteria	US	California/ Sierra Madre	March			city park	"largest blooming plant in the world" (500' branches), Wisteria Festival; scented
wisteria	US	Georgia/ Savannah	mid- to late April		covering trees	city wide	scented

Country	Location	Bloom Time	Flowers	Cultivated	Wild	Garden	Notes
ylang ylang trees	Caribbean	throughout	August to October		humid lowlands		scented
ylang ylang trees	Madagascar	Nosy Be	most of year	plantation			scented
ylang ylang trees	Philippines	throughout	most of year		humid lowlands	city wide	scented
ylang ylang trees	US	Hawaii	August to October		humid lowlands	gardens, parks	scented

My *FLOWERtripping*™ Notes

Afterword

FLOWERtripping™ A Traveler's Guide to What's Blooming When is designed as an itinerary- planning tool for travelers. As such, there are three aspects of the data that may need clarification:

1) The use of the common names of flowers rather than their botanical names.
2) The absence of listing species and varieties of flowers.
3) The choice of locations.

1) The use of the common names of flowers rather than their botanical names.

My reasoning for preferring common plant names to their Latin botanical names is simple: *FLOWERtrippers* are travelers first. They want to view plants in bloom for the effect on their senses, on the scene before them, and on their memories of the trip. Seeing the beauty of flowers, whether a single blossom or a whole field in bloom, enhances their experiences.

For example, when *FLOWERtrippers* return home from a trip to Alaska in June and describe the small blue flowers blooming in the meadows to their friends, they'll most likely say the meadows were filled with forget-me-nots. It provides an easily understood picture to their listeners. Describing the same scene using the Latin botanical name for forget-me-nots, Myosotis, probably won't convey the same image— unless their listeners are botanists.

2) The absence of listing species and varieties of flowers.

FLOWERtripping™ is designed for itinerary research, not flower identification. So, with a few exceptions, I have refrained from listing varieties of flowers, and sometimes species, in the data. This "macro lens" approach refers mainly to the large flower genera found in this book: rhododendron, orchid, and rose.

For the purposes of travelers, including references to certain species of rhododendron or roses does not seem to make traveling to see the plant in bloom any more of a priority. For example, azaleas bloom in North and South Carolina from February to April; this is what interests *FLOWERtrippers.* The several subgenus and varieties of azalea that bloom there are beyond the intent of this book (but you can find out when you visit!).

However, some flowers, knowing when a particular species blooms is important. Take lilies as an example. Each species is unique enough to warrant timing a trip just to see it in bloom: Easter lilies are found in their place of origin, Bermuda; Guernsey lilies flower in quantity in the Channel Isles; and Madonna lilies grow profusely in Madeira.

Readers wanting to view a particular species of orchid, perhaps in its place of origin or natural habitat, will research that orchid and travel to see it in bloom. For example, the largest orchid species in the world (Grammatophyllum speciosum) blooms in the lowland rainforest of Malaysia in September.

My focus on keeping the data in *FLOWERtripping*™ user-friendly for travelers extends to my use of the terms "wildflowers" and "alpine wildflowers." These terms bring a certain image to our minds—that of quantity and diversity in a naturally bordered landscape. Although a field of wildflowers contains individual and unique flowers, it creates an effect as a whole. They are like a tapestry: if you separate out the various species of flowers, you lose the essence of the whole and the tapestry falls apart.

3) The choice of locations.

Since flowers exist on every continent except Antarctica, choosing which ones best served *FLOWERtrippers* was an exercise in restraint. I kept in mind that travelers must balance where to go with what to see and when to see it. Some great places have been left out simply because I had to stop somewhere. Needless to say, a reference guide like this one requires updating. So, send me your *FLOWERtripping*™ experiences and we'll add it to the next edition! (See eNewsletter for contact information.)

Receive the free eNewsleter *FLOWERtripper!*

FLOWERtrippers need to be kept up-to-date with what's happening around the world regarding flowers. We don't want to arrive at our destination and hear, "Oh, you should have been here last week—you just missed the flowers!"

Purchase a book and receive a free monthly emailed eNewsletter, *FLOWERtripper!* **which includes:**

- Information about famous flower shows and flower markets (with contact info and links).
- Botanical or garden tours.
- Timely itinerary information on bloom times for wildflowers and flower field crops around the world.
- Unusual blooming times or unusual flowers.
- Trip preparation including, setting trip goals, exercise before and during your travels, pre-trip health boost, packing, travel gadgets and gear, etc.
- Maintaining your health while you're traveling, journal and photography tips, travel sketching, journaling, etc.
- Travel book reviews.
- Announcements of upcoming *FLOWERtripping*™ Tours.
- Quotes from travelers about travel.

- Information from other *FLOWERtrippers* on what flowers they've discovered from their travels.

To receive this free monthly eNewsletter, email the information below to: kate@flowertripping.com (You may unsubscribe at any time.)

First name ______________________ Last name ________________________________

Email address ____

Your flower discoveries:

Guidebooks and the Internet are effective up to a point in destination research, but there's no substitute for direct information from recent travelers to influence specific aspects of your itinerary. As a *FLOWERtripper!* you return from your travels with current information on the flowers you saw on your trip and if you share your discoveries with other *FLOWERtrippers*, I will print them in the newsletter and give you credit.

This is what I'll need from you:

- Where were you?
- What month were you there?
- What was blooming?
- Why did it impress you?
- Your name, as you want it to appear in the *FLOWERtripper!* eNewsletter.

Email your submission to:
kate@flowertripping.com

About the Author

FLOWERtripping™ A Traveler's Guide to What's Blooming When is a result of author Kate Savory's frustration when designing an itinerary for a worldwide trip that included seeing flowers in bloom.

While degrees in history and art history fueled a passion for world travel, it was Kate's 25-year vocation as an herbalist that focused her interests in flowers. She owned and operated an herb farm south of Rochester, New York for nine years and then a medicinal herb store in Scottsdale, Arizona for two years.

More recently, Kate has been a successful ghostwriter with her own business, A Savory Word. She also has a travel destination research business called, Why Go There? She teaches travel workshops for women and travels whenever and wherever she can.

Kate Savory
PO Box 1353, Chico, CA 95927
(530) 899-8217
kate@flowertripping.com
www.flowertripping.com

FLOWERtripping™ Tours
TOURS

Want to see flowers in bloom on your next trip?

Join Kate Savory on FLOWERtripping™ Tours around the world!

Machu Picchu
Turkey
Madeira
Japan
Tasmania
Iceland
China
Australia
Cape Town, South Africa
New Zealand

These are just some of the places we'll go!

Scheduled for 2007 and arranged by a local travel agency, these tours will visit selected international destinations during peak bloom times.

For more information, email:
kate@flowertripping.com

Tired, achy feet?
Too much sitting, walking, standing?

FOOT OIL for *FLOWERtripping*™

PERFECT FOR THE TRAVELER!

Directions: Massage into clean, dry feet for relief from too much walking or standing. For best results, apply at bedtime. *(Warning: Not for use in pregnancy.)*

A custom-designed topical oil with four essential oils traditionally known for their therapeutic and rejuvenating effects on the tissues and fluids in the feet.

In just one application this unique formula:

- moves the lymph that pools in your feet after too much standing or traveling.
- returns the blood back to the legs and rejuvenates your soles, arches, and tops of your feet.
- refreshes your feet with a cooling effect from one of the oils.
- makes your feet happy and allows you to keep traveling!

2 oz $4.95 + shipping: $3.55 = $8.50
4 oz $9.95 + shipping: $3.55 = $13.50

This proprietary blend is excellent for travelers after sitting on airplanes and in cars, standing in theme park lines and museums, walking on cobblestones and pavement, and long hikes.

"Your foot oil kept me going every day in all the museums in Paris!"
– Margaret VanLaanMartin, Age of Aquarius, Chico, CA

"I never hike anywhere without your foot oil!"
– Carol W., Grand Junction, CO

FOOT OIL for *FLOWERtripping*™

Created in 1994 by Kate Savory, herbalist since 1980.

Only available from

www.flowertripping.com and www.as avoryword.com

HOW TO ORDER

A Traveler's Guide to What's Blooming When

Available now $19.95 each

- Downloadable eBook (pdf)
- Paperback book
- eBook on CD

(for paperback and CD add $3.50 shipping)

MC/Visa accepted

To order, see our website: www.flowertripping.com

Or email me: kate@flowertripping.com

GARDEN TOUR COMPANIES

Aroma Tours
www.aroma-tours.com

Botanical Tours
www.naturetrek.co.uk

Carlson Wagonlit Travel
www.gardenersworldtours.com

Eco Family Botanical Tours
www.eco-family.com

Expo Garden Tours
www.expogardentours.com

Jeff Sainsbury Tours
www.jeffsainsburytours.com

Gardens Guide
www.gardenvisit.com

Great Garden Tours
www.greatgardentours.com

Horticulture Magazine
www.hortmag.com

Natural History Travel
www.gibbonsr.fslife.co.uk

Sejours in Flora n Fauna
www.sejours-ff.com

Tours Gallery Japan
www.toursgallery.com

My *FLOWERtripping*™ Notes